D0298163

# HENRY WADSWORTH LONGFELLOW

## Selected Poems

BLOOM SBURY
* POETRY *
CLASSICS

This selection by Ian Hamilton
First published 1999

Copyright © 1999 by Bloomsbury Publishing Plc

Bloomsbury Publishing Plc, 38 Soho Square,
London W1V 5DF

A CIP catalogue record for this book
is available from the British Library

ISBN 0 7475 4686 X

10 9 8 7 6 5 4 3 2 1

Typeset in Great Britain by
Hewer Text Limited, Edinburgh
Printed in Great Britain by St Edmundsbury Press, Suffolk
Jacket design by Jeff Fisher

# CONTENTS

# POSSIBILITIES

Where are the Poets, unto whom belong
   The Olympian heights; whose singing shafts were sent
   Straight to the mark, and not from bows half bent,
   But with the utmost tension of the thong?
Where are the stately argosies of song,
   Whose rushing keels made music as they went
   Sailing in search of some new continent,
   With all sail set, and steady winds and strong?
Perhaps there lives some dreamy boy, untaught
   In schools, some graduate of the field or street,
   Who shall become a master of the art,
An admiral sailing the high seas of thought,
   Fearless and first and steering with his fleet
   For lands not yet laid down in any chart.

# A PSALM OF LIFE

What the heart of the young man said to the psalmist

Tell me not, in mournful numbers,
  'Life is but an empty dream!'
For the soul is dead that slumbers,
  And things are not what they seem.

Life is real! Life is earnest!
  And the grave is not its goal;
'Dust thou art, to dust returnest,'
  Was not spoken of the soul.

Not enjoyment, and not sorrow,
  Is our destined end or way;
But to act, that each to-morrow
  Finds us farther than to-day.

Art is long, and Time is fleeting.
  And our hearts, though stout and brave,
Still, like muffled drums, are beating
  Funeral marches to the grave.

In the world's broad field of battle,
  In the bivouac of Life,
Be not like dumb, driven cattle!
  Be a hero in the strife!

Trust no Future, howe'er pleasant!
   Let the dead Past bury its dead!
Act, – act in the living Present!
   Heart within, and God o'erhead!

Lives of great men all remind us
   We can make our lives sublime,
And, departing, leave behind us
   Footprints on the sands of time;

Footprints, that perhaps another,
   Sailing o'er life's solemn main,
A forlorn and shipwrecked brother,
   Seeing, shall take heart again.

Let us, then, be up and doing,
   With a heart for any fate;
Still achieving, still pursuing,
   Learn to labour and to wait.

# THE INDIAN HUNTER

When the summer harvest was gather'd in,
And the sheaf of the gleaner grew white and thin,
And the ploughshare was in its furrow left,
Where the stubble land had been lately cleft,
An Indian hunter, with unstrung bow,
Look'd down where the valley lay stretch'd below.

He was a stranger there, and all that day,
Had been out on the hills, a perilous way,
But the foot of the deer was far and fleet,
And the wolf kept aloof from the hunter's feet,
And bitter feelings pass'd o'er him then,
As he stood by the populous haunts of men.

The winds of autumn came over the woods
As the sun stole out from their solitudes,
The moss was white on the maple's trunk,
And dead from its arms the pale vine shrunk,
And ripen'd the mellow fruit hung, and red
Were the tree's wither'd leaves round it shed.

The foot of the reaper moved slow on the lawn,
And the sickle cut down the yellow corn, –
The mower sung loud by the meadow-side,
Where the mists of evening were spreading wide,
And the voice of the herdsman came up the lea,
And the dance went round by the greenwood tree.

Then the hunter turn'd away from that scene,
Where the home of his fathers once had been,
And heard by the distant and measured stroke,
That the woodman hew'd down the giant oak,
And burning thoughts flash'd over his mind,
Of the white man's faith, and love unkind.

The moon of the harvest grew high and bright,
As her golden horn pierced the cloud of white, –
A footstep was heard in the rustling brake,
Where the beech overshadow'd the misty lake,
And a mourning voice, and a plunge from the shore; –
And the hunter was seen on the hills no more.

When years had pass'd on, by that still lake-side
The fisher look'd down through the silver tide,
And there on the smooth yellow sand display'd,
A skeleton wasted and white was laid,
And 'twas seen, as the waters moved deep and slow,
That the hand was still grasping a hunter's bow.

# BURIAL OF THE MINNISINK

On sunny slope and beechen swell,
The shadowed light of evening fell;
And, where the maple's leaf was brown,
With soft and silent lapse came down
The glory, that the wood receives,
At sunset, in its brazen leaves.

Far upward in the mellow light
Rose the blue hills. One cloud of white,
Around a far uplifted cone,
In the warm blush of evening shone;
An image of the silver lakes,
By which the Indian's soul awakes.

But soon a funeral hymn was heard
Where the soft breath of evening stirred
The tall, gray forest; and a band
Of stern in heart, and strong in hand,
Came winding down beside the wave,
To lay the red chief in his grave.

They sang, that by his native bowers
He stood, in the last moon of flowers,
And thirty snows had not yet shed
Their glory on the warrior's head;
But, as the summer fruit decays,
So died he in those naked days.

A dark cloak of the roebuck's skin
Covered the warrior, and within
Its heavy folds the weapons, made
For the hard toils of war, were laid;
The cuirass, woven of plaited reeds,
And the broad belt of shells and beads.

Before, a dark-haired virgin train
Chanted the death dirge of the slain;
Behind, the long procession came
Of hoary men and chiefs of fame,
With heavy hearts, and eyes of grief,
Leading the war-horse of their chief.

Stripped of his proud and martial dress,
Uncurbed, unreined, and riderless,
With darting eye, and nostril spread,
And heavy and impatient tread,
He came; and oft that eye so proud
Asked for his rider in the crowd.

They buried the dark chief, they freed
Beside the grave his battle steed;
And swift an arrow cleaved its way
To his stern heart! One piercing neigh
Arose, – and, on the dead man's plain,
The rider grasps his steed again.

# THE WRECK OF THE HESPERUS

It was the schooner Hesperus,
  That sailed the wintry sea;
And the skipper had taken his little daughtèr,
  To bear him company.

Blue were her eyes as the fairy-flax,
  Her cheeks like the dawn of day,
And her bosom white as the hawthorn buds
  That ope in the month of May.

The skipper he stood beside the helm,
  His pipe was in his mouth,
And he watched how the veering flaw did blow
  The smoke now West, now South.

Then up and spake an old Sailòr,
  Had sailed the Spanish Main,
'I pray thee, put into yonder port,
  For I fear a hurricane.

'Last night the moon had a golden ring,
  And to-night no moon we see!'
The skipper he blew a whiff from his pipe,
  And a scornful laugh laughed he.

Colder and colder blew the wind,
  A gale from the North-east;
The snow fell hissing in the brine,
  And the billows frothed like yeast.

Down came the storm, and smote amain,
  The vessel in its strength;
She shuddered and paused, like a frightened steed,
  Then leaped her cable's length.

'Come hither! come hither! my little daughtèr,
  And do not tremble so;
For I can weather the roughest gale,
  That ever wind did blow.'

He wrapped her warm in his seaman's coat
  Against the stinging blast;
He cut a rope from a broken spar,
  And bound her to the mast.

'O father! I hear the church-bells ring,
  O say, what may it be?'
' 'Tis a fog-bell on a rock-bound coast!' –
  And he steered for the open sea.

'O father! I hear the sound of guns,
  O say, what may it be?'
'Some ship in distress, that cannot live
  In such an angry sea!'

'O father! I see a gleaming light,
  O say, what may it be?'
But the father answered never a word,
  A frozen corpse was he.

Lashed to the helm, all stiff and stark,
  With his face turned to the skies,
The lantern gleamed through the gleaming snow
  On his fixed and glassy eyes.

Then the maiden clasped her hands and prayed
  That savèd she might be;
And she thought of Christ, who stilled the wave,
  On the Lake of Galilee.

And fast through the midnight dark and drear,
  Through the whistling sleet and snow,
Like a sheeted ghost, the vessel swept
  Towards the reef of Norman's Woe.

And ever the fitful gusts between
  A sound came from the land;
It was the sound of the trampling surf,
  On the rocks and the hard sea-sand.

The breakers were right beneath her bows,
  She drifted a dreary wreck,
And a whooping billow swept the crew
  Like icicles from her deck.

She struck where the white and fleecy waves
    Looked soft as carded wool,
But the cruel rocks, they gored her side
    Like the horns of an angry bull.

Her rattling shrouds, all sheathed in ice,
    With the masts went by the board;
Like a vessel of glass, she stove and sank,
    Ho! ho! the breakers roared!

At daybreak, on the bleak sea-beach,
    A fisherman stood aghast,
To see the form of a maiden fair,
    Lashed close to a drifting mast.

The salt sea was frozen on her breast,
    The salt tears in her eyes;
And he saw her hair, like the brown sea-weed,
    On the billows fall and rise.

Such was the wreck of the Hesperus,
    In the midnight and the snow!
Christ save us all from a death like this
    On the reef of Norman's Woe!

# THE VILLAGE BLACKSMITH

Under a spreading chestnut tree
   The village smithy stands;
The smith, a mighty man is he,
   With large and sinewy hands;
And the muscles of his brawny arms
   Are strong as iron bands.

His hair is crisp, and black, and long,
   His face is like the tan;
His brow is wet with honest sweat,
   He earns whate'er he can,
And looks the whole world in the face,
   For he owes not any man.

Week in, week out, from morn till night,
   You can hear his bellows blow;
You can hear him swing his heavy sledge,
   With measured beat and slow,
Like a sexton ringing the village bell,
   When the evening sun is low.

And children coming home from school
   Look in at the open door;
They love to see the flaming forge,
   And hear the bellows roar,
And catch the burning sparks that fly
   Like chaff from a threshing floor.

He goes on Sunday to the church,
　And sits among his boys;
He hears the parson pray and preach,
　He hears his daughter's voice,
Singing in the village choir,
　And it makes his heart rejoice.

It sounds to him like her mother's voice,
　Singing in Paradise!
He needs must think of her once more,
　How in the grave she lies;
And with his hard, rough hand he wipes
　A tear out of his eyes.

Toiling, – rejoicing, – sorrowing,
　Onward through life he goes;
Each morning sees some task begin,
　Each evening sees it close;
Something attempted, something done,
　Has earned a night's repose.

Thanks, thanks to thee, my worthy friend,
　For the lesson thou hast taught!
Thus at the flaming forge of life
　Our fortunes must be wrought;
Thus on its sounding anvil shaped
　Each burning deed and thought!

# THE RAINY DAY

The day is cold, and dark, and dreary;
It rains, and the wind is never weary;
The vine still clings to the mouldering wall,
But at every gust the dead leaves fall,
    And the day is dark and dreary.

My life is cold, and dark, and dreary;
It rains, and the wind is never weary;
My thoughts still cling to the mouldering Past,
But the hopes of youth fall thick in the blast,
    And the days are dark and dreary.

Be still, sad heart! and cease repining;
Behind the clouds is the sun still shining;
Thy fate is the common fate of all,
Into each life some rain must fall,
    Some days must be dark and dreary.

# THE BUILDING OF THE SHIP

'Build me straight, O worthy Master!
  Staunch and strong, a goodly vessel,
That shall laugh at all disaster,
  And with wave and whirlwind wrestle!'

The merchant's word
Delighted the Master heard;
For his heart was in his work, and the heart
Giveth grace unto every Art.
A quiet smile played round his lips,
As the eddies and dimples of the tide
Play round the bows of ships,
That steadily at anchor ride.
And with a voice that was full of glee,
He answered, 'Ere long we will launch
A vessel as goodly, and strong, and staunch,
As ever weathered a wintry sea!'

And first with nicest skill and art,
Perfect and finished in every part,
A little model the Master wrought,
Which should be to the larger plan
What the child is to the man,
Its counterpart in miniature;
That with a hand more swift and sure
The greater labour might be brought
To answer to his inward thought.

And as he laboured, his mind ran o'er
The various ships that were built of yore,
And above them all, and strangest of all
Towered the Great Harry, crank and tall,
Whose picture was hanging on the wall,
With bows and stern raised high in air,
And balconies hanging here and there,
And signal lanterns and flags afloat,
And eight round towers, like those that frown
From some old castle, looking down
Upon the drawbridge and the moat.
And he said with a smile, 'Our ship, I wis,
Shall be of another form than this!'

It was of another form, indeed;
Built for freight, and yet for speed,
A beautiful and gallant craft;
Broad in the beam, that the stress of the blast
Pressing down upon sail and mast,
Might not the sharp bows overwhelm;
Broad in the beam, but sloping aft
With graceful curve and slow degrees,
That she might be docile to the helm
And that the currents of parted seas,
Closing behind, with mighty force,
Might aid and not impede her course.

In the shipyard stood the Master,
  With the model of the vessel,
That should laugh at all disaster,
  And with wave and whirlwind wrestle!

Covering many a rood of ground,
Lay the timber piled around;
Timber of chestnut and elm and oak,
And scattered here and there, with these,
The knarred and crooked cedar knees;
Brought from regions far away,
From Pascagoula's sunny bay,
And the banks of the roaring Roanoke!
Oh! what a wondrous thing it is
To note how many wheels of toil
One thought, one word, can set in motion!
There's not a ship that sails the ocean,
But every climate, every soil,
Must bring its tribute, great or small,
And help to build the wooden wall!

The sun was rising o'er the sea,
And long the level shadows lay,
As if they, too, the beams would be
Of some great, airy argosy,
Framed and launched in a single day.
That silent architect, the sun,
Had hewn and laid them every one,
Ere the work of man was yet begun.

Beside the Master, when he spoke,
A youth, against an anchor leaning
Listened, to catch his slightest meaning.
Only the long waves, as they broke
In ripples on the pebbly beach,
Interrupted the old man's speech.
Beautiful they were, in sooth,
The old man and the fiery youth!
The old man, in whose busy brain
Many a ship that sailed the main
Was modelled o'er and o'er again; –
The fiery youth, who was to be
The heir of his dexterity,
The heir of his house, and his daughter's hand,
When he had built and launched from land
What the elder head had planned.

'Thus,' said he, 'will we build this ship!
Lay square the blocks upon the slip,
And follow well this plan of mine.
Choose the timbers with greatest care;
Of all that is unsound beware;
For only what is sound and strong
To this vessel shall belong.
Cedar of Maine and Georgia pine
Here together shall combine.
A goodly frame, and a goodly fame,
And the Union be her name!

For the day that gives her to the sea
Shall give my daughter unto thee!'
The Master's word
Enraptured the young man heard;
And as he turned his face aside,
With a look of joy and a thrill of pride
Standing before
Her father's door,
He saw the form of his promised bride.

The sun shone on her golden hair,
And her cheek was glowing fresh and fair,
With the breath of morn and the soft sea air.
Like a beauteous barge was she,
Still at rest on the sandy beach,
Just beyond the billow's reach;
But he
Was the restless, seething, stormy sea!

Ah, how skilful grows the hand
That obeyeth Love's command!
It is the heart and not the brain,
That to the highest doth attain,
And he who followeth Love's behest
Far exceedeth all the rest!
Thus with the rising of the sun
Was the noble task begun,
And soon throughout the shipyard's bounds
Were heard the intermingled sounds

Of axes and of mallets, plied
With vigorous arms on every side;
Plied so deftly and so well,
That, ere the shadows of evening fell,
The keel of oak for a noble ship,
Scarfed and bolted, straight and strong,
Was lying ready, and stretched along
The blocks, well placed upon the slip.
Happy, thrice happy, every one
Who sees his labour well begun,
And not perplexed and multiplied,
By idly waiting for time and tide!

And when the hot, long day was o'er,
The young man at the Master's door
Sat with the maiden calm and still.
And within the porch, a little more
Removed beyond the evening chill,
The father sat, and told them tales
Of wrecks in the great September gales,
Of pirates upon the Spanish Main,
And ships that never came back again,
The chance and change of a sailor's life,
Want and plenty, rest and strife,
His roving fancy, like the wind,
That nothing can stay and nothing can bind,
And the magic charm of foreign lands,
With shadows of palms, and shining sands,
Where the tumbling surf,

O'er the coral reefs of Madagascar,
Washes the feet of the swarthy Lascar,
As he lies alone and asleep on the turf.
And the trembling maiden held her breath
At the tales of that awful, pitiless sea,
With all its terror and mystery,
The dim, dark sea, so like unto Death,
That divides and yet unites mankind!
And whenever the old man paused, a gleam
From the bowl of his pipe would awhile illume
The silent group in the twilight gloom,
And thoughtful faces, as in a dream;
And for a moment one might mark
What had been hidden by the dark,
That the head of the maiden lay at rest,
Tenderly, on the young man's breast!

Day by day the vessel grew,
With timbers fashioned strong and true,
Stemson and keelson and sternson-knee,
Till, framed with perfect symmetry,
A skeleton ship rose up to view!
All around the bows and along the side
The heavy hammers and mallets plied,
Till, after many a week, at length,
Wonderful for form and strength,
Sublime in its enormous bulk,
Loomed aloft the shadowy hulk!

And around it columns of smoke, upwreathing,
Rose from the boiling, bubbling, seething
Caldron, that glowed,
And overflowed
With the black tar, heated for the sheathing.
And amid the clamours
Of clattering hammers,
He who listened heard now and then
The song of the Master and his men: –

'Build me straight, O worthy Master,
    Staunch and strong, a goodly vessel,
That shall laugh at all disaster,
    And with wave and whirlwind wrestle!'

With oaken brace and copper band,
Lay the rudder on the sand,
That, like a thought, should have control
Over the movement of the whole;
And near it the anchor, whose giant hand
Would reach down and grapple with the land,
And immovable and fast
Hold the great ship against the bellowing blast!
And at the bows an image stood,
By a cunning artist carved in wood,
With robes of white, that far behind
Seemed to be fluttering in the wind.
It was not shaped in a classic mould,
Not like a Nymph or Goddess of old,

Or Naiad rising from the water,
But modelled from the Master's daughter!
On many a dreary and misty night,
'Twill be seen by the rays of the signal light,
Speeding along through the rain and the dark,
Like a ghost in its snow-white sark,
The pilot of some phantom bark,
Guiding the vessel, in its flight,
By a path none other knows aright!
Behold, at last
Each tall and tapering mast
Is swung into its place;
Shrouds and stays
Holding it firm and fast!

Long ago,
In the deer-haunted forests of Maine,
When upon mountain and plain
Lay the snow,
They fell, – those lordly pines!
Those grand, majestic pines!
Mid shouts and cheers
The jaded steers,
Panting beneath the goad,
Dragged down the weary, winding road
Those captive kings so straight and tall.
To be shorn of their streaming hair,
And, naked and bare,

To feel the stress and the strain
Of the wind and the reeling main,
Whose roar
Would remind them for evermore
Of their native forests they should not see again.

And everywhere
The slender, graceful spars
Poise aloft in the air,
And at the mast-head,
White, blue, and red,
A flag unrolls the stripes and stars.
Ah! when the wanderer, lonely, friendless,
In foreign harbours shall behold
That flag unrolled,
'Twill be as a friendly hand
Stretched out from his native land,
Filling his heart with memories sweet and endless!

All is finished! and at length
Has come the bridal day
Of beauty and of strength.
To-day the vessel shall be launched!
With fleecy clouds the sky is blanched,
And o'er the bay,
Slowly, in all his splendours dight,
The great sun rises to behold the sight.

The ocean old,
Centuries old,
Strong as youth, and as uncontrolled,
Paces restless to and fro,
Up and down the sands of gold.
His beating heart is not at rest;
And far and wide,
With ceaseless flow,
His beard of snow
Heaves with the heaving of his breast.
He waits impatient for his bride.
There she stands,
With her foot upon the sands,
Decked with flags and streamers gay,
In honour of her marriage day,
Her snow-white signals fluttering, blending,
Round her like a veil descending,
Ready to be
The bride of the gray, old sea.

On the deck another bride
Is standing by her lover's side.
Shadows from the flags and shrouds,
Like the shadows cast by clouds,
Broken by many a sunny fleck,
Fall around them on the deck.

The prayer is said,
The service read,
The joyous bridegroom bows his head.
And in tears the good old Master
Shakes the brown hand of his son,
Kisses his daughter's glowing cheek
In silence, for he cannot speak,
And ever faster
Down his own the tears begin to run.
The worthy pastor –
The shepherd of that wandering flock,
That has the ocean for its wold,
That has the vessel for its fold,
Leaping ever from rock to rock –
Spake, with accents mild and clear,
Words of warning, words of cheer,
But tedious to the bridegroom's ear.

He knew the chart
Of the sailor's heart,
All its pleasures and its griefs,
All its shallows and rocky reefs,
All those secret currents, that flow
With such resistless undertow,
And lift and drift, with terrible force,
The will from its moorings and its course,
Therefore he spake, and thus said he: –
'Like unto ships far off at sea,
Outward or homeward bound, are we.

Before, behind and all around,
Floats and swings the horizon's bound,
Seems at its distant rim to rise
And climb the crystal wall of the skies,
And then again to turn and sink,
As if we could slide from its outer brink.
Ah! it is not the sea,
It is not the sea that sinks and shelves,
But ourselves
That rock and rise
With endless and uneasy motion,
Now touching the very skies,
Now sinking into the depths of ocean.
Ah! if our souls but poise and swing
Like the compass in its brazen ring,
Ever level and ever true
To the toil and the task we have to do,
We shall sail securely, and safely reach
The Fortunate Isles, on whose shining beach
The sights we see, and the sounds we hear,
Will be those of joy and not of fear!'

Then the Master,
With a gesture of command,
Waved his hand;
And at the word,
Loud and sudden there was heard,
All around them and below,
The sound of hammers, blow on blow,

Knocking away the shores and spurs.
And see! she stirs!
She starts, – she moves, – she seems to feel
The thrill of life along her keel,
And, spurning with her foot the ground,
With one exulting, joyous, bound,
She leaps into the ocean's arms!
And lo! from the assembled crowd
There rose a shout, prolonged and loud,
That to the ocean seemed to say, –
'Take her, O bridegroom, old and gray,
Take her to thy protecting arms,
With all her youth and all her charms!'
How beautiful she is! How fair
She lies within those arms, that press
Her form with many a soft caress
Of tenderness and watchful care!
Sail forth into the sea, O ship!
Through wind and wave, right onward steer!
The moistened eye, the trembling lip,
Are not the signs of doubt or fear.
Sail forth into the sea of life,
O gentle, loving, trusting wife,
And safe from all adversity
Upon the bosom of that sea
Thy comings and thy goings be!
For gentleness and love and trust
Prevail o'er angry wave and gust;
And in the wreck of noble lives
Something immortal still survives!

Thou, too, sail on, O Ship of State!
Sail on, O UNION, strong and great!
Humanity with all its fears,
With all the hopes of future years,
Is hanging breathless on thy fate!
We know what Master laid thy keel,
What Workmen wrought thy ribs of steel,
Who made each mast, and sail, and rope,
What anvils rang, what hammers beat,
In what a forge and what a heat
Were shaped the anchors of thy hope!
Fear not each sudden sound and shock,
'Tis of the wave and not the rock;
'Tis but the flapping of the sail,
And not a rent made by the gale!
In spite of rock and tempest's roar,
In spite of false lights on the shore,
Sail on, nor fear to breast the sea!
Our hearts, our hopes, are all with thee,
Our hearts, our hopes, our prayers, our tears,
Our faith triumphant o'er our fears,
Are all with thee, – are all with thee!

# THE TIDES

I saw the long line of the vacant shore,
   The sea-weed and the shells upon the sand,
   And the brown rocks left bare on every hand,
   As if the ebbing tide would flow no more.
Then heard I, more distinctly than before,
   The ocean breathe and its great breast expand,
   And hurrying came on the defenceless land
   The insurgent waters with tumultuous roar.
All thought and feeling and desire, I said,
   Love, laughter, and the exultant joy of song
   Have ebbed from me for ever! Suddenly o'er me
They swept again from their deep ocean bed,
   And in a tumult of delight, and strong
   As youth, and beautiful as youth, upbore me.

# THE BRIDGE

I stood on the bridge at midnight,
  As the clocks were striking the hour,
And the moon rose o'er the city,
  Behind the dark church-tower.

I saw her bright reflection
  In the waters under me,
Like a golden goblet falling
  And sinking into the sea.

And far in the hazy distance
  Of that lovely night in June,
The blaze of the flaming furnace
  Gleamed redder than the moon.

Among the long, black rafters
  The waving shadows lay,
And the current that came from the ocean
  Seemed to lift and bear them away;

As, sweeping and eddying through them,
  Rose the belated tide,
And, streaming into the moonlight,
  The seaweed floated wide.

And like those waters rushing
   Among the wooden piers,
A flood of thoughts came o'er me
   That filled my eyes with tears.

How often, O, how often,
   In the days that had gone by,
I had stood on that bridge at midnight,
   And gazed on that wave and sky!

How often, O, how often,
   I had wished that the ebbing tide
Would bear me away on its bosom
   O'er the ocean wild and wide!

For my heart was hot and restless,
   And my life was full of care,
And the burden laid upon me
   Seemed greater than I could bear.

But now it has fallen from me,
   It is buried in the sea;
And only the sorrow of others
   Throws its shadow over me.

Yet whenever I cross the river
   On its bridge with wooden piers,
Like the odour of brine from the ocean
   Comes the thought of other years.

And I think how many thousands
  Of care-encumbered men,
Each bearing his burden of sorrow,
  Have crossed the bridge since then.

I see the long procession
  Still passing to and fro,
The young heart hot and restless,
  And the old subdued and slow!

And for ever and for ever,
  As long as the river flows,
As long as the heart has passions,
  As long as life has woes;

The moon and its broken reflection
  And its shadows shall appear,
As the symbol of love in heaven,
  And its waving image here.

## THE FIRE OF DRIFT-WOOD

We sat within the farmhouse old,
  Whose windows, looking o'er the bay,
Gave to the sea-breeze, damp and cold,
  An easy entrance, night and day.

Not far away we saw the port, –
  The strange, old-fashioned, silent town, –
The lighthouse, – the dismantled fort, –
  The wooden houses, quaint and brown.

We sat and talked until the night,
  Descending, filled the little room;
Our faces faded from the sight,
  Our voices only broke the gloom.

We spake of many a vanished scene,
  Of what we once had thought and said,
Of what had been, and might have been,
  And who was changed, and who was dead.

And all that fills the hearts of friends,
  When first they feel, with secret pain,
Their lives thenceforth have separate ends,
  And never can be one again;

The first slight swerving of the heart,
    That words are powerless to express,
And leave it still unsaid in part,
    Or say it in too great excess.

The very tones in which we spake
    Had something strange, I could but mark;
The leaves of memory seemed to make
    A mournful rustling in the dark.

Oft died the words upon our lips,
    As suddenly, from out the fire
Built of the wreck of stranded ships,
    The flames would leap and then expire.

And, as their splendour flashed and failed,
    We thought of wrecks upon the main, –
Of ships dismasted, that were hailed
    And sent no answer back again.

The windows, rattling in their frames, –
    The ocean, roaring up the beach, –
The gusty blast, – the bickering flames, –
    All mingled vaguely in our speech;

Until they made themselves a part
    Of fancies floating through the brain,
The long-lost ventures of the heart,
    That send no answers back again.

O flames that glowed! O hearts that yearned!
　　They were indeed too much akin,
The drift-wood fire without that burned,
　　The thoughts that burned and glowed within.

# THE TWO ANGELS

Two angels, one of Life and one of Death,
   Passed o'er our village as the morning broke;
The dawn was on their faces, and beneath,
   The sombre houses hearsed with plumes of smoke.

Their attitude and aspect were the same,
   Alike their features and their robes of white;
But one was crowned with amaranth, as with flame,
   And one with asphodels, like flakes of light.

I saw them pause on their celestial way;
   Then said I, with deep fear and doubt oppressed,
'Beat not so loud, my heart, lest thou betray
   The place where thy beloved are at rest!'

And he who wore the crown of asphodels,
   Descending, at my door began to knock,
And my soul sank within me, as in wells
   The waters sink before an earthquake's shock.

I recognised the nameless agony,
   The terror and the tremor and the pain,
That oft before had filled or haunted me,
   And now returned with threefold strength again.

The door I opened to my heavenly guest,
  And listened, for I thought I heard God's voice;
And, knowing whatsoe'er he sent was best,
  Dared neither to lament nor to rejoice.

Then with a smile, that filled the house with light,
  'My errand is not Death, but Life,' he said;
And ere I answered, passing out of sight,
  On his celestial embassy he sped.

'Twas at thy door, O friend! and not at mine,
  The angel with the amaranthine wreath,
Pausing, descended, and with voice divine,
  Whispered a word that had a sound like Death.

Then fell upon the house a sudden gloom,
  A shadow on those features fair and thin;
And softly, from that hushed and darkened room,
  Two angels issued, where but one went in.

All is of God! If he but wave his hand,
  The mists collect, the rain falls thick and loud,
Till, with a smile of light on sea and land,
  Lo! he looks back from the departing cloud.

Angels of Life and Death alike are his;
  Without his leave they pass no threshold o'er;
Who, then, would wish or dare, believing this,
  Against his messengers to shut the door?

## PAUL REVERE'S RIDE

Listen, my children, and you shall hear
Of the midnight ride of Paul Revere,
On the eighteenth of April, in Seventy-five;
Hardly a man is now alive
Who remembers that famous day and year.

He said to his friend, 'If the British march
By land or sea from the town to-night,
Hang a lantern aloft in the belfry arch
Of the North Church tower as a signal light, –
One, if by land, and two, if by sea;
And I on the opposite shore will be,
Ready to ride and spread the alarm
Through every Middlesex village and farm,
For the country folk to be up and to arm.'

Then he said, 'Good night!' and with muffled oar
Silently rowed to the Charlestown shore,
Just as the moon rose over the bay,
Where swinging wide at her moorings lay
The Somerset, British man-of-war;
A phantom ship, with each mast and spar
Across the moon like a prison bar,
And a huge black hulk, that was magnified
By its own reflection in the tide.

Meanwhile, his friend, through alley and street,
Wanders and watches with eager ears,
Till in the silence around him he hears
The muster of men at the barrack door,
The sound of arms, and the tramp of feet,
And the measured tread of the grenadiers,
Marching down to their boats on the shore.

Then he climbed the tower of the Old North Church,
By the wooden stairs, with stealthy tread,
To the belfry-chamber overhead,
And startled the pigeons from their perch
On the sombre rafters, that round him made
Masses and moving shapes of shade, –
By the trembling ladder, steep and tall,
To the highest window in the wall,
Where he paused to listen and look down
A moment on the roofs of the town,
And the moonlight flowing over all.

Beneath, in the churchyard, lay the dead,
In their night-encampment on the hill,
Wrapped in silence so deep and still
That he could hear, like a sentinel's tread,
The watchful night-wind, as it went
Creeping along from tent to tent,
And seeming to whisper, 'All is well!'
A moment only he feels the spell
Of the place and the hour, and the secret dread
Of the lonely belfry and the dead;

For suddenly all his thoughts are bent
On a shadowy something far away,
Where the river widens to meet the bay, –
A line of black that bends and floats
On the rising tide, like a bridge of boats.

Meanwhile, impatient to mount and ride,
Booted and spurred, with a heavy stride
On the opposite shore walked Paul Revere.
Now he patted his horse's side,
Now gazed at the landscape far and near,
Then, impetuous, stamped the earth,
And turned and tightened his saddle-girth;
But mostly he watched with eager search
The belfry-tower of the Old North Church,
As it rose above the graves on the hill,
Lonely and spectral and sombre and still.
And lo! as he looks, on the belfry's height
A glimmer, and then a gleam of light!
He springs to the saddle, the bridle he turns,
But lingers and gazes, till full on his sight
A second lamp in the belfry burns!

A hurry of hoofs in a village street,
A shape in the moonlight, a bulk in the dark,
And beneath, from the pebbles, in passing, a spark
Struck out by a steed flying fearless and fleet:
That was all! And yet, through the gloom and the
    light,

The fate of a nation was riding that night;
And the spark struck out by that steed, in his flight,
Kindled the land into flame with its heat.

He has left the village and mounted the steep,
And beneath him, tranquil and broad and deep,
Is the Mystic, meeting the ocean tides;
And under the alders, that skirt its edge,
Now soft on the sand, now loud on the ledge,
Is heard the tramp of his steed as he rides.

It was twelve by the village clock
When he crossed the bridge into Medford town.
He heard the crowing of the cock,
And the barking of the farmer's dog,
And felt the damp of the river fog,
That rises after the sun goes down.

It was one by the village clock,
When he galloped into Lexington.
He saw the gilded weathercock
Swim in the moonlight as he passed,
And the meeting-house windows, blank and bare,
Gaze at him with a spectral glare,
As if they already stood aghast
At the bloody work they would look upon.

It was two by the village clock,
When he came to the bridge in Concord town.
He heard the bleating of the flock,

And the twitter of birds among the trees,
And felt the breath of the morning breeze
Blowing over the meadows brown.
And one was safe and asleep in his bed
Who at the bridge would be first to fall,
Who that day would be lying dead,
Pierced by a British musket-ball.

You know the rest. In the books you have read,
How the British Regulars fired and fled, –
How the farmers gave them ball for ball,
From behind each fence and farmyard wall,
Chasing the red-coats down the lane,
Then crossing the fields to emerge again
Under the trees at the turn of the road,
And only pausing to fire and load.

So through the night rode Paul Revere;
And so through the night went his cry of alarm
To every Middlesex village and farm, –
A cry of defiance and not of fear,
A voice in the darkness, a knock at the door,
And a word that shall echo for evermore!
For, borne on a night-wind of the Past,
Through all our history, to the last,
In the hour of darkness and peril and need,
The people will waken and listen to hear
The hurrying hoof-beats of that steed,
And the midnight message of Paul Revere.

# AFTERMATH

When the Summer fields are mown,
When the birds are fledged and flown,
  And the dry leaves strew the path;
With the falling of the snow,
With the cawing of the crow,
Once again the fields we mow
  And gather in the aftermath.

Not the sweet, new grass with flowers
Is this harvesting of ours;
  Not the upland clover bloom;
But the rowen mixed with weeds,
Tangled tufts from marsh and meads,
Where the poppy drops its seeds
  In the silence and the gloom.

# THE BUILDERS

All are architects of Fate,
   Working in these walls of Time;
Some with massive deeds and great,
   Some with ornaments of rhyme.

Nothing useless is, or low;
   Each thing in its place is best;
And what seems but idle show
   Strengthens and supports the rest.

For the structure that we raise,
   Time is with materials filled;
Our to-days and yesterdays
   Are the blocks with which we build.

Truly shape and fashion these;
   Leave no yawning gaps between;
Think not, because no man sees,
   Such things will remain unseen.

In the elder days of Art,
   Builders wrought with greatest care
Each minute an unseen part;
   For the Gods see everywhere.

Let us do our work as well,
    Both the unseen and the seen!
Make the house, where Gods may dwell,
    Beautiful, entire, and clean.

Else our lives are incomplete,
    Standing in these walls of Time,
Broken stairways, where the feet
    Stumble as they seek to climb.

Build to-day, then, strong and sure,
    With a firm and ample base;
And ascending and secure
    Shall to-morrow find its place.

Thus alone can we attain
    To those turrets, where the eye
Sees the world as one vast plain,
    And one boundless reach of sky.

# THE JEWISH CEMETERY AT NEWPORT

How strange it seems! These Hebrews in their graves,
   Close by the street of this fair seaport town.
Silent beside the never-silent waves,
   At rest in all this moving up and down!

The trees are white with dust, that o'er their sleep
   Wave their broad curtains in the south-wind's breath,
While underneath such leafy tents they keep
   The long, mysterious Exodus of Death.

And these sepulchral stones, so old and brown,
   That pave with level flags their burial-place,
Seem like the tablets of the Law, thrown down
   And broken by Moses at the mountain's base.

The very names recorded here are strange,
   Of foreign accent, and of different climes:
Alvares and Rivera interchange
   With Abraham and Jacob of old times.

'Blessed be God! for he created Death!'
   The mourners said, 'and Death is rest and peace';
Then added, in the certainty of faith,
   'And giveth Life that never more shall cease.'

Closed are the portals of their Synagogue,
  No Psalms of David now the silence break,
No Rabbi reads the ancient Decalogue
  In the grand dialect the Prophets spake.

Gone are the living, but the dead remain,
  And not neglected; for a hand unseen,
Scattering its bounty, like a summer rain,
  Still keeps their graves and their remembrance green.

How came they here? What burst of Christian hate,
  What persecution, merciless and blind,
Drove o'er the sea – that desert desolate –
  These Ishmaels and Hagars of mankind?

They lived in narrow streets and lanes obscure,
  Ghetto and Judenstrass, in mirk and mire;
Taught in the school of patience to endure
  The life of anguish and the death of fire.

All their lives long, with the unleavened bread
  And bitter herbs of exile and its fears,
The wasting famine of the heart they fed,
  And slaked its thirst with marah of their tears.

Anathema marantha! was the cry
  That rang from town to town, from street to street;
At every gate the accursed Mordecai
  Was mocked and jeered, and spurned by Christian feet.

Pride and humiliation hand in hand
    Walked with them through the world where'er they went;
Trampled and beaten were they as the sand,
    And yet unshaken as the continent.

For in the background figures vague and vast
    Of patriarchs and prophets rose sublime,
And all the great traditions of the Past
    They saw reflected in the coming time.

And thus for ever with reverted look
    The mystic volume of the world they read,
Spelling it backward, like a Hebrew book.
    Till life became a Legend of the Dead.

But ah! what once has been shall be no more!
    The groaning earth in travail and in pain
Brings forth its races, but does not restore,
    And the dead nations never rise again.

INTRODUCTION

Should you ask me, whence these stories?
Whence these legends and traditions,
With the odours of the forest,
With the dew and damp of meadows,
With the curling smoke of wigwams,
With the rushing of great rivers,
With their frequent repetitions,
And their wild reverberations,
As of thunder in the mountains?
  I should answer, I should tell you,
'From the forests and the prairies,
From the great lakes of the Northland,
From the land of the Ojibways,
From the land of the Dacotahs,
From the mountains, moors, and fenlands,
Where the heron, the Shuh-shuh-gah,
Feeds among the reeds and rushes.
I repeat them as I heard them
From the lips of Nawadaha,
The musician, the sweet singer.'
  Should you ask where Nawadaha
Found these songs, so wild and wayward,
Found these legends and traditions,
I should answer, I should tell you,
'In the birds'-nests of the forest,

In the lodges of the beaver,
In the hoof-prints of the bison,
In the eyrie of the eagle!

'All the wild-fowl sang them to him,
In the moorlands and the fenlands,
In the melancholy marshes;
Chetowaik, the plover, sang them,
Mahng, the loon, the wild-goose, Wawa,
The blue heron, the Shuh-shuh-gah,
And the grouse, the Mushkodasa!'

If still further you should ask me,
Saying, 'Who was Nawadaha?
Tell us of this Nawadaha,'
I should answer your inquiries
Straightway in such words as follow:

'In the Vale of Tawasentha,
In the green and silent valley,
By the pleasant water-courses,
Dwelt the singer Nawadaha.
Round about the Indian village
Spread the meadows and the cornfields,
And beyond them stood the forest,
Stood the groves of singing pine-trees,
Green in Summer, white in Winter,
Ever sighing, ever singing.

'And the pleasant water-courses,
You could trace them through the valley,
By the rushing in the Spring-time,
By the alders in the Summer,

By the white fog in the Autumn,
By the black line in the Winter;
And beside them dwelt the singer,
In the Vale of Tawasentha,
In the green and silent valley.

'There he sang of Hiawatha,
Sang the Song of Hiawatha,
Sang his wondrous birth and being,
How he prayed and how he fasted,
How he lived, and toiled, and suffered,
That the tribes of men might prosper,
That he might advance his people!'

Ye who love the haunts of Nature,
Love the sunshine of the meadow,
Love the shadow of the forest,
Love the wind among the branches,
And the rain-shower and the snow-storm,
And the rushing of great rivers
Though their palisades of pine-trees,
And the thunder in the mountains,
Whose innumerable echoes
Flap like eagles in their eyries; –
Listen to these wild traditions,
To this Song of Hiawatha!

Ye who love a nation's legends,
Love the ballads of a people,
That like voices from afar off
Call to us to pause and listen,
Speak in tones so plain and childlike,

Scarcely can the ear distinguish
Whether they are sung or spoken; –
Listen to this Indian Legend,
To this Song of Hiawatha!

Ye whose hearts are fresh and simple,
Who have faith in God and Nature,
Who believe, that in all ages
Every human heart is human,
That in even savage bosoms
There are longings, yearnings, strivings
For the good they comprehend not,
That the feeble hands and helpless,
Groping blindly in the darkness,
Touch God's right hand in that darkness
And are lifted up and strengthened; –
Listen to this simple story,
To this Song of Hiawatha!

Ye, who sometimes in your rambles
Through the green lanes of the country,
Where the tangled barberry-bushes
Hang their tufts of crimson berries
Over stone walls gray with mosses,
Pause by some neglected graveyard,
For a while to muse, and ponder
On a half-effaced inscription,
Written with little skill of song-craft, –
Homely phrases, but each letter
Full of hope and yet of heart-break,
Full of all the tender pathos

Of the Here and the Hereafter; –
Stay and read this rude inscription,
Read this Song of Hiawatha!

## IV.

### *Hiawatha and Mudjekeewis*

Out of childhood into manhood
Now had grown my Hiawatha,
Skilled in all the craft of hunters,
Learned in all the lore of old men,
In all youthful sports and pastimes,
In all manly arts and labours.

Swift of foot was Hiawatha;
He could shoot an arrow from him,
And run forward with such fleetness,
That the arrow fell behind him!
Strong of arm was Hiawatha;
He could shoot ten arrows upward,
Shoot them with such strength and swiftness,
That the tenth had left the bowstring
Ere the first to earth had fallen!

He had mittens, Minjekahwun,
Magic mittens made of deerskin;
When upon his hands he wore them,
He could smite the rocks asunder,
He could grind them into powder.
He had moccasins enchanted,
Magic moccasins of deerskin;
When he bound them round his ankles,
When upon his feet he tied them,

At each stride a mile he measured!
　　Much he questioned old Nokomis
Of his father Mudjekeewis;
Learned from her the fatal secret
Of the beauty of his mother,
Of the falsehood of his father;
And his heart was hot within him,
Like a living coal his heart was.

　　Then he said to old Nokomis,
'I will go to Mudjekeewis,
See how fares it with my father,
At the doorways of the West-Wind,
At the portals of the Sunset!'
　　From his lodge went Hiawatha,
Dressed for travel, armed for hunting;
Dressed in deerskin shirt and leggings,
Richly wrought with quills and wampum;
On his head his eagle-feathers,
Round his waist his belt or wampum,
In his hand his bow of ash-wood,
Strung with sinews of the reindeer;
In his quiver oaken arrows,
Tipped with jasper, winged with feathers;
With his mittens, Minjekahwun,
With his moccasins enchanted.

　　Warning said the old Nokomis,
'Go not forth, O Hiawatha!
To the kingdom of the West-Wind,
To the realms of Mudjekeewis,

Lest he harm you with his magic,
Lest he kill you with his cunning!'
   But the fearless Hiawatha
Heeded not her woman's warning;
Forth he strode into the forest,
At each stride a mile he measured;
Lurid seemed the sky above him,
Lurid seemed the earth beneath him,
Hot and close the air around him,
Filled with smoke and fiery vapours,
As of burning woods and prairies,
For his heart was hot within him,
Like a living coal his heart was.

   So he journeyed westward, westward,
Left the fleetest deer behind him,
Left the antelope and bison;
Crossed the rushing Esconaba,
Crossed the mighty Mississippi,
Passed the Mountains of the Prairie,
Passed the land of Crows and Foxes,
Passed the dwellings of the Blackfeet,
Came unto the Rocky Mountains,
To the kingdom of the West-Wind,
Where upon the gusty summits
Sat the ancient Mudjekeewis,
Ruler of the winds of heaven.

   Filled with awe was Hiawatha
At the aspect of his father.
On the air about him wildly

Tossed and streamed his cloudy tresses,
Gleamed like drifting snow his tresses,
Glared like Ishkoodah, the comet,
Like the star with fiery tresses.

Filled with joy was Mudjekeewis
When he looked on Hiawatha,
Saw his youth rise up before him
In the face of Hiawatha,
Saw the beauty of Wenonah
From the grave rise up before him.

'Welcome!' said he, 'Hiawatha,
To the kingdom of the West-Wind!
Long have I been waiting for you!
Youth is lovely, age is lonely,
Youth is fiery, age is frosty;
You bring back the days departed,
You bring back my youth of passion,
And the beautiful Wenonah!'

Many days they talked together,
Questioned, listened, waited, answered;
Much the mighty Mudjekeewis
Boasted of his ancient prowess,
Of his perilous adventures,
His indomitable courage,
His invulnerable body.

Patiently sat Hiawatha,
Listening to his father's boasting;
With a smile he sat and listened,
Uttered neither threat nor menace,

Neither word nor look betrayed him;
But his heart was hot within him,
Like a living coal his heart was.

Then he said, 'O Mudjekeewis,
Is there nothing that can harm you?
Nothing that you are afraid of?'
And the might Mudjekeewis,
Grand and gracious in his boasting,
Answered, saying, 'There is nothing,
Nothing but the black rock yonder,
Nothing but the fatal Wawbeek!'

And he looked at Hiawatha
With a wise look and benignant,
With a countenance paternal,
Looked with pride upon the beauty
Of his tall and graceful figure,
Saying, 'O my Hiawatha!
Is there anything can harm you?
Anything you are afraid of?'

But the wary Hiawatha
Paused a while, as if uncertain,
Held his peace, as if resolving,
And then answered, 'There is nothing,
Nothing but the bulrush yonder,
Nothing but the great Apukwa!'

And as Mudjekeewis, rising,
Stretched his hand to pluck the bulrush,
Hiawatha cried in terror,
Cried in well-dissembled terror,

'Kago! kago! do not touch it!'
'Ah, kaween!' said Mudjekeewis,
'No indeed, I will not touch it!'

Then they talked of other matters;
First of Hiawatha's brothers,
First of Wabun, of the East-Wind,
Of the South-Wind, Shawondasee,
Of the North, Kabibonokka;
Then of Hiawatha's mother,
Of the beautiful Wenonah,
Of her birth upon the meadow,
Of her death, as old Nokomis
Had remembered and related.

And he cried, 'O Mudjekeewis,
It was you who killed Wenonah,
Took her young life and her beauty,
Broke the Lily of the Prairie,
Trampled it beneath your footsteps;
You confess it! you confess it!'
And the mighty Mudjekeewis
Tossed upon the wind his tresses,
Bowed his hoary head in anguish,
With a silent nod assented.

Then upstarted Hiawatha,
And with threatening look and gesture
Laid his hand upon the black rock,
On the fatal Wawbeek laid it,
With his mittens, Minjekahwun,
Rent the jutting crag asunder,

Smote and crushed it into fragments,
Hurled them madly at his father,
The remorseful Mudjekeewis;
For his heart was hot within him,
Like a living coal his heart was.

But the ruler of the West-Wind
Blew the fragments backward from him,
With the breathing of his nostrils,
With the tempest of his anger,
Blew them back at his assailant;
Seized the bulrush, the Apukwa,
Dragged it with its roots and fibres
From the margin of the meadow,
From its ooze, the giant bulrush;
Long and loud laughed Hiawatha!

Then began the deadly conflict,
Hand to hand among the mountains;
From his eyrie screamed the eagle,
The Keneu, the great war-eagle;
Sat upon the crags around them,
Wheeling flapped his wings above them.

Like a tall tree in the tempest
Bent and lashed the giant bulrush;
And in masses huge and heavy
Crashing fell the fatal Wawbeek;
Till the earth shook with the tumult
And confusion of the battle,
And the air was full of shoutings,
And the thunder of the mountains,

Starting, answered, 'Baim-wawa!'
Back retreated Mudjekeewis,
Rushing westward o'er the mountains,
Stumbling westward down the mountains,
Three whole days retreated fighting,
Still pursued by Hiawatha
To the doorways of the West-Wind,
To the portals of the Sunset,
To the earth's remotest border,
Where into the empty spaces
Sinks the sun, as a flamingo
Drops into her nest at nightfall,
In the melancholy marshes.

'Hold!' at length cried Mudjekeewis,
'Hold, my son, my Hiawatha!
'Tis impossible to kill me,
For you cannot kill the immortal.
I have put you to this trial,
But to know and prove your courage;
Now receive the prize of valour!

'Go back to your home and people,
Live among them, toil among them,
Cleanse the earth from all that harms it,
Clear the fishing-grounds and rivers,
Slay all monsters and magicians,
All the Wendigoes, the giants,
All the serpents, the Kenabeeks,
As I slew the Mishe-Mokwa,
Slew the Great Bear of the mountains.

'And at last when Death draws near you,
When the awful eyes of Pauguk
Glare upon you in the darkness,
I will share my kingdom with you;
Ruler shall you be thenceforward
Of the Northwest-Wind, Keewaydin,
Of the home-wind, the Keewaydin.'

Thus was fought that famous battle
In the dreadful days of Shah-shah,
In the days long since departed,
In the kingdom of the West-Wind.
Still the hunter sees its traces
Scattered far o'er hill and valley;
Sees the giant bulrush growing
By the ponds and water-courses,
Sees the masses of the Wawbeek
Lying still in every valley.

Homeward now went Hiawatha;
Pleasant was the landscape round him,
Pleasant was the air above him,
For the bitterness of anger
Had departed wholly from him,
From his brain the thought of vengeance,
From his heart the burning fever.

Only once his pace he slackened,
Only once he paused or halted,
Paused to purchase heads of arrows
Of the ancient Arrow-maker,
In the land of the Dacotahs,

Where the Falls of Minnehaha
Flash and gleam among the oak-trees,
Laugh and leap into the valley.

There the ancient Arrow-maker
Made his arrow-heads of sandstone,
Arrow-heads of chalcedony,
Arrow-heads of flint and jasper,
Smoothed and sharpened at the edges,
Hard and polished, keen and costly.

With him dwelt his dark-eyed daughter,
Wayward as the Minnehaha,
With her moods of shade and sunshine,
Eyes that smiled and frowned alternate,
Feet as rapid as the river,
Tresses flowing like the water,
And as musical a laughter;
And he named her from the river,
From the waterfall he named her,
Minnehaha, Laughing Water.

Was it then for heads of arrows,
Arrow-heads of chalcedony,
Arrow-heads of flint and jasper,
That my Hiawatha halted
In the land of the Dacotahs?

Was it not to see the maiden,
See the face of Laughing Water
Peeping from behind the curtain,
Hear the rustling of her garments
From behind the waving curtain,

As one sees the Minnehaha
Gleaming, glancing through the branches,
As one hears the Laughing Water
From behind its screen of branches?
   Who shall say what thoughts and visions
Fill the fiery brains of young men?
Who shall say what dreams of beauty
Filled the heart of Hiawatha?
All he told to old Nokomis,
When he reached the lodge at sunset,
Was the meeting with his father,
Was his fight with Mudjekeewis;
Not a word he said of arrows,
Not a word of Laughing Water.

## X.

### *Hiawatha's Wooing*

'As unto the bow the cord is,
So unto the man is woman,
Though she bends him, she obeys him,
Though she draws him, yet she follows,
Useless each without the other!'

Thus the youthful Hiawatha
Said within himself and pondered,
Much perplexed by various feelings,
Listless, longing, hoping, fearing,
Dreaming still of Minnehaha,
Of the lovely Laughing Water,
In the land of the Dacotahs.

'Wed a maiden of your people,'
Warning said the old Nokomis;
'Go not eastward, go not westward,
For a stranger, whom we know not!
Like a fire upon the hearthstone
Is a neighbour's homely daughter;
Like the starlight or the moonlight
Is the handsomest of strangers!'

Thus dissuading spake Nokomis,
And my Hiawatha answered
Only this: 'Dear old Nokomis,
Very pleasant is the firelight,

But I like the starlight better,
Better do I like the moonlight!'
    Gravely then said old Nokomis:
'Bring not here an idle maiden,
Bring not here a useless woman,
Hands unskilful, feet unwilling;
Bring a wife with nimble fingers.
Heart and hand that move together,
Feet that run on willing errands!'
    Smiling answered Hiawatha:
'In the land of the Dacotahs
Lives the Arrow-maker's daughter,
Minnehaha, Laughing Water,
Handsomest of all the women.
I will bring her to your wigwam,
She shall run upon your errands,
Be your starlight, moonlight, firelight,
Be the sunlight of my people!'
    Still dissuading said Nokomis:
'Bring not to my lodge a stranger
From the land of the Dacotahs!
Very fierce are the Dacotahs,
Often is there war between us,
There are feuds yet unforgotten,
Wounds that ache and still may open!'
    Laughing answered Hiawatha:
'For that reason, if no other,
Would I wed the fair Dacotah,
That our tribes might be united,

That old feuds might be forgotten,
And old wounds be healed for ever!'
　　Thus departed Hiawatha
To the land of the Dacotahs,
To the land of handsome women;
Striding over moor and meadow,
Through interminable forests,
Through uninterrupted silence.

　　With his moccasins of magic,
At each stride a mile he measured;
Yet the way seemed long before him,
And his heart outran his footsteps;
And he journeyed without resting,
Till he heard the cataract's laughter,
Heard the Falls of Minnehaha
Calling to him through the silence.
'Pleasant is the sound!' he murmured,
'Pleasant is the voice that calls me!'

　　On the outskirts of the forest,
'Twixt the shadow and the sunshine,
Herds of fallow deer were feeding,
But they saw not Hiawatha;
To his bow he whispered, 'Fail not!'
To his arrow whispered, 'Swerve not!'
Sent it singing on its errand,
To the red heart of the roebuck;
Threw the deer across his shoulder,
And sped forward without pausing.

　　At the doorway of his wigwam

Sat the ancient Arrow-maker,
In the land of the Dacotahs,
Making arrow-heads of jasper,
Arrow-heads of chalcedony.
At his side, in all her beauty,
Sat the lovely Minnehaha,
Sat his daughter, Laughing Water,
Plaiting mats of flags and rushes;
Of the past the old man's thoughts were,
And the maiden's of the future.

He was thinking, as he sat there,
Of the days when with such arrows
He had struck the deer and bison,
On the Muskoday, the meadow;
Shot the wildgoose, flying southward,
On the wing, the clamorous Wawa;
Thinking of the great war-parties,
How they came to buy his arrows,
Could not fight without his arrows.
Ah, no more such noble warriors
Could be found on earth as they were!
Now the men were all like women,
Only used their tongues for weapons!

She was thinking of a hunter,
From another tribe and country,
Young and tall and very handsome,
Who one morning in the Spring-time
Came to buy her father's arrows,
Sat and rested in the wigwam,

Lingered long about the doorway,
Looking back as he departed.
She had heard her father praise him,
Praise his courage and his wisdom;
Would he come again for arrows
To the Falls of Minnehaha?
On the mat her hands lay idle,
And her eyes were very dreamy.

Through their thoughts they heard a footstep,
Heard a rustling in the branches,
And with glowing cheek and forehead,
With the deer upon his shoulders,
Suddenly from out the woodlands
Hiawatha stood before them.

Straight the ancient Arrow-maker
Looked up gravely from his labour,
Laid aside the unfinished arrow,
Bade him enter at the doorway,
Saying, as he rose to meet him,
'Hiawatha, you are welcome!'

At the feet of Laughing Water
Hiawatha laid his burden,
Threw the red deer from his shoulders;
And the maiden looked up at him,
Looked up from her mat of rushes,
Said with gentle look and accent,
'You are welcome, Hiawatha!'

Very spacious was the wigwam,
Made of deerskin dressed and whitened,

With the Gods of the Dacotahs
Drawn and painted on its curtains,
And so tall the doorway, hardly
Hiawatha stooped to enter,
Hardly touched his eagle-feathers
As he entered at the doorway.

   Then uprose the Laughing Water,
From the ground fair Minnehaha,
Laid aside her mat unfinished,
Brought forth food and set before them,
Water brought them from the brooklet,
Gave them food in earthen vessels,
Gave them drink in bowls of bass-wood,
Listened while the guest was speaking,
Listened while her father answered;
But not once her lips she opened,
Not a single word she uttered.

   Yes, as in a dream she listened
To the words of Hiawatha,
As he talked of old Nokomis,
Who had nursed him in his childhood,
As he told of his companions,
Chibiabos, the musician,
And the very strong man, Kwasind,
And of happiness and plenty
In the land of the Ojibways,
In the pleasant land and peaceful.

   'After many years of warfare,
Many years of strife and bloodshed,

There is peace between the Ojibways
And the tribe of the Dacotahs.'
Thus continued Hiawatha,
And then added, speaking slowly,
'That this peace may last for ever,
And our hands be clasped more closely,
And our hearts be more united,
Give me as my wife this maiden,
Minnehaha, Laughing Water,
Loveliest of Dacotah women!'

And the ancient Arrow-maker
Paused a moment ere he answered,
Smoked a little while in silence,
Looked at Hiawatha proudly,
Fondly looked at Laughing Water,
And made answer very gravely:
'Yes, if Minnehaha wishes;
Let your heart speak, Minnehaha!'

And the lovely Laughing Water
Seemed more lovely, as she stood there,
Neither willing nor reluctant,
As she went to Hiawatha,
Softly took the seat beside him,
While she said, and blushed to say it,
'I will follow you, my husband!'

This was Hiawatha's wooing!
Thus it was he won the daughter
Of the ancient Arrow-maker,
In the land of the Dacotahs!

From the wigwam he departed,
Leading with him Laughing Water;
Hand in hand they went together,
Through the woodland and the meadow,
Left the old man standing lonely
At the doorway of his wigwam,
Heard the Falls of Minnehaha
Calling to them from the distance,
Crying to them from afar off,
'Fare thee well, O Minnehaha!'

And the ancient Arrow-maker
Turned again unto his labour,
Sat down by his sunny doorway,
Murmuring to himself, and saying:
'Thus it is our daughters leave us,
Those we love, and those who love us!
Just when they have learned to help us,
When we are old and lean upon them,
Comes a youth with flaunting feathers,
With his flute of reeds, a stranger
Wanders piping through the village,
Beckons to the fairest maiden,
And she follows where he leads her,
Leaving all things for the stranger!'

Pleasant was the journey homeward,
Through interminable forests,
Over meadow, over mountain,
Over river, hill, and hollow.
Short it seemed to Hiawatha,

Though they journeyed very slowly,
Though his pace he checked and slackened
To the steps of Laughing Water.

Over wide and rushing rivers
In his arms he bore the maiden;
Light he thought her as a feather,
As the plume upon his head-gear;
Cleared the tangled pathway for her,
Bent aside the swaying branches,
Made at night a lodge of branches,
And a bed with boughs of hemlock,
And a fire before the doorway
With the dry cones of the pine-tree.

All the travelling winds went with them,
O'er the meadow, through the forest;
All the stars of night looked at them,
Watched with sleepless eyes their slumber;
From his ambush in the oak-tree
Peeped the squirrel, Adjidaumo,
Watched with eager eyes the lovers;
And the rabbit, the Wabasso,
Scampered from the path before them,
Peering, peeping from his burrow,
Sat erect upon his haunches,
Watched with curious eyes the lovers.

Pleasant was the journey homeward!
All the birds sang loud and sweetly
Songs of happiness and heart's-ease;
Sang the bluebird, the Owaissa,

'Happy are you, Hiawatha,
Having such a wife to love you!'
Sang the robin, the Opechee,
'Happy are you, Laughing Water,
Having such a noble husband!'

From the sky the sun benignant
Looked upon them through the branches,
Saying to them, 'O my children,
Love is sunshine, hate is shadow,
Life is checkered shade and sunshine,
Rule by love, O Hiawatha!'

From the sky the moon looked at them,
Filled the lodge with mystic splendours,
Whispered to them, 'O my children,
Day is restless, night is quiet,
Man imperious, woman feeble;
Half is mine, although I follow;
Rule by patience, Laughing Water!'

Thus it was they journeyed homeward;
Thus it was that Hiawatha
To the lodge of old Nokomis
Brought the moonlight, starlight, firelight,
Brought the sunshine of his people,
Minnehaha, Laughing Water,
Handsomest of all the women
In the land of the Dacotahs,
In the land of handsome women.

*From* THE SONG OF HIAWATHA

## XV.
### *Hiawatha's Lamentation*

In those days the Evil Spirits,
All the Manitos of mischief,
Fearing Hiawatha's wisdom,
And his love for Chibiabos,
Jealous of their faithful friendship,
And their noble words and actions,
Made at length a league against them,
To molest them and destroy them.

   Hiawatha, wise and wary,
Often said to Chibiabos,
'O my brother! do not leave me,
Lest the Evil Spirits harm you!'
Chibiabos, young and heedless,
Laughing shook his coal-black tresses,
Answered ever sweet and childlike,
'Do not fear for me, O brother!
Harm and evil come not near me!'

   Once when Peboan, the Winter,
Roofed with ice the Big-Sea-Water,
When the snow-flakes, whirling downward,
Hissed among the withered oak-leaves,
Changed the pine-trees into wigwams,
Covered all the earth with silence, –
Armed with arrows, shod with snow-shoes,

Heeding not his brother's warning,
Fearing not the Evil Spirits,
Forth to hunt the deer with antlers
All alone went Chibiabos.

Right across the Big-Sea-Water
Sprang with speed the deer before him.
With the wind and snow he followed,
O'er the treacherous ice he followed,
Wild with all the fierce commotion
And the rapture of the hunting.

But beneath, the Evil Spirits
Lay in ambush, waiting for him,
Broke the treacherous ice beneath him,
Dragged him downward to the bottom,
Buried in the sand his body.
Unktahee, the god of water,
He the god of the Dacotahs,
Drowned him in the deep abysses
Of the lake of Gitche Gumee.

From the headlands Hiawatha
Sent forth such a wail of anguish,
Such a fearful lamentation,
That the bison paused to listen,
And the wolves howled from the prairies,
And the thunder in the distance
Starting answered 'Baim-wawa!'

Then his face with black he painted,
With his robe his head he covered,
In his wigwam sat lamenting,

Seven long weeks he sat lamenting,
Uttering still this moan of sorrow: –
   'He is dead, the sweet musician!
He the sweetest of all singers!
He has gone from us for ever,
He has moved a little nearer
To the Master of all music,
To the Master of all singing!
O my brother, Chibiabos!'

   And the melancholy fir-trees
Waved their dark green fans above him,
Waved their purple cones above him,
Sighing with him to console him,
Mingling with his lamentation
Their complaining, their lamenting.

   Came the Spring, and all the forest
Looked in vain for Chibiabos;
Sighed the rivulet, Sebowisha,
Sighed the rushes in the meadow.

   From the tree-tops sang the bluebird,
Sang the bluebird, the Owaissa,
'Chibiabos! Chibiabos!
He is dead, the sweet musician!'

   From the wigwam sang the robin,
Sang the robin, the Opechee,
'Chibiabos! Chibiabos!
He is dead, the sweetest singer!'

   And at night through all the forest
Went the whippoorwill complaining,

Wailing went the Wawonaissa,
'Chibiabos! Chibiabos!
He is dead, the sweet musician!'
He the sweetest of all singers!'
    Then the medicine-men, the Medas,
The magicians, the Wabenos,
And the Jossakeeds, the prophets,
Came to visit Hiawatha;
Built a Sacred Lodge beside him,
To appease him, to console him,
Walked in silent grave procession,
Bearing each a pouch of healing,
Skin of beaver, lynx, or otter,
Filled with magic roots and simples,
Filled with very potent medicines.
    When he heard their steps approaching,
Hiawatha ceased lamenting,
Called no more on Chibiabos;
Naught he questioned, naught he answered,
But his mournful head uncovered,
From his face the mourning colours
Washed he slowly and in silence,
Slowly and in silence followed
Onward to the Sacred Wigwam.
    There a magic drink they gave him,
Made of Nahma-wusk, the spearmint,
And Wabeno-wusk, the yarrow,
Roots of power, and herbs of healing;
Beat their drums, and shook their rattles;

Chanted singly and in chorus,
Mystic songs like these, they chanted.

'I myself, myself! behold me!
'Tis the great Gray Eagle talking;
Come, ye white crows, come and hear him!
The loud-speaking thunder helps me;
All the unseen spirits help me;
I can hear their voices calling,
All around the sky I hear them!
I can blow you strong, my brother,
I can heal you, Hiawatha!'

'Hi-au-ha!' replied the chorus,
'Way-ha-way!' the mystic chorus.

'Friends of mine are all the serpents!
Hear me shake my skin of hen-hawk!
Mahng, the white loon, I can kill him;
I can shoot your heart and kill it!
I can blow you strong, my brother,
I can heal you, Hiawatha!'

'Hi-au-ha!' replied the chorus,
'Way-ha-way!' the mystic chorus.

'I myself, myself! the prophet!
When I speak the wigwam trembles,
Shakes the Sacred Lodge with terror,
Hands unseen begin to shake it!
When I walk, the sky I tread on
Bends and makes a noise beneath me!
I can blow you strong, my brother!
Rise and speak, O Hiawatha!'

'Hi-au-ha!' replied the chorus,
'Way-ha-way!' the mystic chorus.

Then they shook their medicine-pouches
O'er the head of Hiawatha,
Danced their medicine-dance around him;
And upstarting wild and haggard,
Like a man from dreams awakened,
He was healed of all his madness.
As the clouds are swept from heaven,
Straightway from his brain departed
All his moody melancholy;
As the ice is swept from rivers,
Straightway from his heart departed
All his sorrow and affliction.

Then they summoned Chibiabos
From his grave beneath the waters,
From the sands of Gitche Gumee
Summoned Hiawatha's brother.
And so mighty was the magic
Of that cry and invocation,
That he heard it as he lay there
Underneath the Big-Sea-Water;
From the sand he rose and listened,
Heard the music and the singing,
Came, obedient to the summons,
To the doorway of the wigwam,
But to enter they forbade him.

Through a chink a coal they gave him,
Through the door a burning fire-brand;

Ruler in the Land of Spirits,
Ruler o'er the dead, they made him,
Telling him a fire to kindle
For all those that died thereafter,
Camp-fires for their night encampments
On their solitary journey
To the kingdom of Ponemah,
To the land of the Hereafter.

From the village of his childhood,
From the homes of those who knew him,
Passing silent through the forest,
Like a smoke-wreath wafted sideways,
Slowly vanished Chibiabos!
Where he passed, the branches moved not,
Where he trod, the grasses bent not,
And the fallen leaves of last year
Made no sound beneath his footsteps.

Four whole days he journeyed onward
Down the pathway of the dead men;
On the dead-man's strawberry feasted,
Crossed the melancholy river,
On the swinging log he crossed it,
Came unto the Lake of Silver,
In the Stone Canoe was carried
To the Islands of the Blessed,
To the land of ghosts and shadows.

On that journey, moving slowly,
Many weary spirits saw he,
Panting under heavy burdens,

Laden with war-clubs, bows and arrows,
Robes of fur, and pots and kettles,
And with food that friends had given
For that solitary journey.
    'Ay! why do the living,' said they,
'Lay such heavy burdens on us!
Better were it to go naked,
Better were it to go fasting,
Than to bear such heavy burdens
On our long and weary journey!'
    Forth then issued Hiawatha,
Wandered eastward, wandered westward,
Teaching men the use of simples
And the antidotes for poisons,
And the cure of all diseases.
Thus was first made known to mortals
All the mystery of Medamin,
All the sacred art of healing.

# EXCELSIOR

The shades of night were falling fast,
As through an Alpine village passed
A youth, who bore, 'mid snow and ice,
A banner with the strange device,
   Excelsior!

His brow was sad; his eye beneath
Flashed like a falchion from its sheath,
And like a silver clarion rung
The accents of that unknown tongue,
   Excelsior!

In happy homes he saw the light
Of household fires gleam warm and bright;
Above, the spectral glaciers shone,
And from his lips escaped a groan,
   Excelsior!

'Try not the Pass!' the old man said;
'Dark lowers the tempest overhead,
The roaring torrent is deep and wide!'
And loud that clarion voice replied,
   Excelsior!

'O stay,' the maiden said, 'and rest
Thy weary head upon this breast!'
A tear stood in his bright blue eye,
But still he answered, with a sigh,
     Excelsior!

'Beware the pine-tree's withered branch!
Beware the awful avalanche!'
This was the peasant's last Goodnight.
A voice replied, far up the height,
     Excelsior!

At break of day, as heavenward
The pious monks of Saint Bernard
Uttered the oft-repeated prayer,
A voice cried through the startled air,
     Excelsior!

A traveller, by the faithful hound,
Half-buried in the snow was found,
Still grasping in his hand of ice
That banner with the strange device,
     Excelsior!

There in the twilight cold and gray,
Lifeless, but beautiful, he lay,
And from the sky, serene and far,
A voice fell, like a falling star,
     Excelsior!

# THE TIDE RISES, THE TIDE FALLS

The tide rises, the tide falls,
The twilight darkens, the curlew calls;
Along the sea-sands damp and brown
The traveller hastens toward the town,
    And the tide rises, the tide falls.

Darkness settles on roofs and walls,
But the sea in the darkness calls and calls;
The little waves, with their soft white hands,
Efface the footprints in the sands,
    And the tide rises, the tide falls.

The morning breaks; the steeds in their stalls
Stamp and neigh, as the hostler calls;
The day returns, but nevermore
Returns the traveller to the shore,
    And the tide rises, the tide falls.

# MEZZO CAMMIN

Half of my life is gone, and I have let
   The years slip from me and have not fulfilled
   The aspiration of my youth, to build
   Some tower of song with lofty parapet.
Not indolence, nor pleasure, nor the fret
   Of restless passions that would not be stilled,
   But sorrow, and a care that almost killed,
   Kept me from what I may accomplish yet;
Though, half-way up the hill, I see the Past
   Lying beneath me with its sounds and sights, –
   A city in the twilight dim and vast,
With smoking roofs, soft bells, and gleaming lights, –
   And hear above me on the autumnal blast
The cataract of Death far thundering from the heights.

# THE DAY IS DONE

The day is done, and the darkness
  Falls from the wings of Night,
As a feather is wafted downward
  From an eagle in his flight.

I see the lights of the village
  Gleam through the rain and the mist,
And a feeling of sadness comes o'er me
  That my soul cannot resist:

A feeling of sadness and longing,
  That is not akin to pain,
And resembles sorrow only
  As the mist resembles the rain.

Come, read to me some poem,
  Some simple and heartfelt lay,
That shall soothe this restless feeling,
  And banish the thoughts of day.

Not from the grand old masters,
  Not from the bards sublime,
Whose distant footsteps echo
  Through the corridors of Time.

For, like strains of martial music,
  Their mighty thoughts suggest
Life's endless toil and endeavor;
  And to-night I long for rest.

Read from some humbler poet,
  Whose songs gushed from his heart,
As showers from the clouds of summer,
  Or tears from the eyelids start;

Who, through long days of labor,
  And nights devoid of ease,
Still heard in his soul the music
  Of wonderful melodies.

Such songs have power to quiet
  The restless pulse of care,
And come like the benediction
  That follows after prayer.

Then read from the treasured volume
  The poem of thy choice,
And lend to the rhyme of the poet
  The beauty of thy voice.

And the night shall be filled with music,
  And the cares, that infest the day,
Shall fold their tents, like the Arabs,
  And as silently steal away.

# NATURE

As fond mother, when the day is o'er
   Leads by the hand her little child to bed,
   Half willing, half reluctant to be led,
   And leave his broken playthings on the floor,
Still gazing at them through the open door,
   Nor wholly reassured and comforted
   By promises of others in their stead,
   Which, though more splendid, may not please him
     more;

So Nature deals with us, and takes away
   Our playthings one by one, and by the hand
   Leads us to rest so gently, that we go
Scarce knowing if we wish to go or stay,
   Being too full of sleep to understand
   How far the unknown transcends the what we know.

# THE CHILDREN'S HOUR

Between the dark and the daylight,
  When the night is beginning to lower,
Comes a pause in the day's occupations,
  That is known as the Children's Hour.

I hear in the chamber above me
  The patter of little feet,
The sound of a door that is opened,
  And voices soft and sweet.

From my study I see in the lamplight,
  Descending the broad hall stair,
Grave Alice, and laughing Allegra,
  And Edith with golden hair.

A whisper, and then a silence:
  Yet I know by their merry eyes
They are plotting and planning together
  To take me by surprise.

A sudden rush from the stairway,
  A sudden raid from the hall!
By three doors left unguarded
  They enter my castle wall!

They climb up into my turret
  O'er the arms and back of my chair;
If I try to escape, they surround me;
  They seem to be everywhere.

They almost devour me with kisses,
    Their arms about me entwine,
Till I think of the Bishop of Bingen
    In his Mouse-Tower on the Rhine!

Do you think, O blue-eyed banditti,
    Because you have scaled the wall,
Such an old mustache as I am
    Is not a match for you all!

I have you fast in my fortress,
    And will not let you depart,
But put you down into the dungeon
    In the round-tower of my heart.

And there will I keep you forever,
    Yes, forever and a day,
Till the walls shall crumble to ruin,
    And moulder in dust away!

# HAUNTED HOUSES

All houses wherein men have lived and died
   Are haunted houses. Through the open doors
The harmless phantoms on their errands glide,
   With feet that make no sound upon the floors.

We meet them at the door-way, on the stair,
   Along the passages they come and go,
Impalpable impressions on the air,
   A sense of something moving to and fro.

There are more guests at table, than the hosts
   Invited; the illuminated hall
Is thronged with quiet, inoffensive ghosts,
   As silent as the pictures on the wall.

The stranger at my fireside cannot see
   The forms I see, nor hear the sounds I hear;
He but perceives what is; while unto me
   All that has been is visible and clear.

We have no title-deeds to house or lands;
   Owners and occupants of earlier dates
From graves forgotten stretch their dusty hands,
   And hold in mortmain still their old estates.

The spirit-world around this world of sense
  Floats like an atmosphere, and everywhere
Wafts through these earthly mists and vapours dense
  A vital breath of more ethereal air.

Our little lives are kept in equipoise
  By opposite attractions and desires;
The struggle of the instinct that enjoys,
  And the more noble instinct that aspires.

These perturbations, this perpetual jar
  Of earthly wants and aspirations high,
Come from the influence of an unseen star,
  An undiscovered planet in our sky.

And as the moon from some dark gate of cloud
  Throws o'er the sea a floating bridge of light,
Across whose trembling planks our fancies crowd,
  Into the realm of mystery and night, –

So from the world of spirits there descends
  A bridge of light, connecting it with this,
O'er whose unsteady floor, that sways and bends,
  Wander our thoughts above the dark abyss.

## II.
### LOVE AND FRIENDSHIP

Nothing was heard in the room but the hurrying pen
  of the stripling,
Or an occasional sigh from the labouring heart of the
  Captain,
Reading the marvellous words and achievements of
  Julius Cæsar.
After a while he exclaimed, as he smote with his hand,
  palm downwards,
Heavily on the page: 'A wonderful man was this
  Cæsar!
You are a writer, and I am a fighter, but here is a fellow
Who could both write and fight, and in both was
  equally skilful!'
Straightway answered and spake John Alden, the
  comely, the youthful:
'Yes, he was equally skilled, as you say, with his pen
  and his weapons.
Somewhere have I read, but where I forget, he could
  dictate
Seven letters at once, at the same time writing his
  memoirs.'
'Truly,' continued the Captain, not heeding or hearing
  the other,
'Truly a wonderful man was Caius Julius Cæsar!

Better be first, he said, in a little Iberian village,
Than be second in Rome, and I think he was right
when he said it.
Twice was he married before he was twenty, and many
times after;
Battles five hundred he fought, and a thousand cities
he conquered;
He, too, fought in Flanders, as he himself has
recorded;
Finally he was stabbed by his friend, the orator Brutus!
Now, do you know what he did on a certain occasion
in Flanders,
When the rear-guard of his army retreated, the front
giving way too,
And the immortal Twelfth Legion was crowded so
closely together
There was no room for their swords? Why, he seized a
shield from a soldier,
Put himself straight at the head of his troops, and
commanded the captains,
Calling on each by his name, to order forward the
ensigns;
Then to widen the ranks, and give more room for
their weapons;
So he won the day, the battle of something-or-other.
That's what I always say; if you wish a thing to be well
done,
You must do it yourself, you must not leave it to
others!'

All was silent again; the Captain continued his reading.

Nothing was heard in the room but the hurrying pen of the stripling

Writing epistles important to go next day by the May Flower,

Filled with the name and the fame of the Puritan maiden Priscilla;

Every sentence began or closed with the name of Priscilla,

Till the treacherous pen, to which he confided the secret,

Strove to betray it by singing and shouting the name of Priscilla!

Finally closing his book, with a bang of the ponderous cover,

Sudden and loud as the sound of a soldier grounding his musket,

Thus to the young man spake Miles Standish the Captain of Plymouth

'When you have finished your work, I have something important to tell you.

Be not however in haste; I can wait; I shall not be impatient!'

Straightway Alden replied, as he folded the last of his letters,

Pushing his papers aside, and giving respectful attention:

'Speak; for whenever you speak, I am always ready to listen,

Always ready to hear whatever pertains to Miles
    Standish.'
Thereupon answered the Captain, embarrassed, and
    culling his phrases:
' 'Tis not good for a man to be alone, say the
    Scriptures.
This have I said before, and again and again I repeat
    it;
Every hour in the day, I think it, and feel it, and say it.
Since Rose Standish died, my life has been weary and
    dreary;
Sick at heart have I been, beyond the healing of
    friendship.
Oft in my lonely hours have I thought of the maiden
    Priscilla.
She is alone in the world; her father and mother and
    brother
Died in the winter together; I saw her going and
    coming,
Now to the grave of the dead, and now to the bed of
    the dying,
Patient, courageous, and strong, and said to myself,
    that if ever
There were angels on earth, as there are angels in
    heaven,
Two have I seen and known; and the angel whose
    name is Priscilla
Holds in my desolate life the place which the other
    abandoned.

Long have I cherished the thought, but never have
    dared to reveal it,
Being a coward in this, though valiant enough for the
    most part.
Go to the damsel Priscilla, the loveliest maiden of
    Plymouth,
Say that a blunt old Captain, a man not of words but
    of actions,
Offers his hand and his heart, the hand and heart of a
    soldier.
Not in these words, you know, but this in short is my
    meaning;
I am a maker of war, and not a maker of phrases.
You, who are bred as a scholar, can say it in elegant
    language,
Such as you read in your books of the pleadings and
    wooings of lovers,
Such as you think best adapted to win the heart of a
    maiden.'

When he had spoken, John Alden, the fair-haired,
    taciturn stripling,
All aghast at his words, surprised, embarrassed, bewildered,
Trying to mask his dismay by treating the subject with
    lightness,
Trying to smile, and yet feeling his heart stand still in
    his bosom,
Just as a timepiece stops in a house that is stricken by
    lightning,

Thus made answer and spake, or rather stammered
than answered:
'Such a message as that, I am sure I should mangle
and mar it;
If you would have it well done, – I am only repeating
your maxim, –
You must do it yourself, you must not leave it to
others!'
But with the air of a man whom nothing can turn
from his purpose,
Gravely shaking his head, made answer the Captain of
Plymouth:
'Truly the maxim is good, and I do not mean to
gainsay it;
But we must use it discreetly, and not waste powder
for nothing.
Now, as I said before, I was never a maker of phrases.
I can march up to a fortress and summon the place to
surrender,
But march up to a woman with such a proposal, I dare
not.
I am not afraid of bullets, nor shot from the mouth of
a cannon,
But of a thundering 'No!' point-blank from the mouth
of a woman,
That I confess I'm afraid of, nor am I ashamed to
confess it!
So you must grant my request, for you are an elegant
scholar,

Having the graces of speech, and skill in the turning of
   phrases.'
Taking the hand of his friend, who still was reluctant
   and doubtful,
Holding it long in his own, and pressing it kindly, he
   added:
'Though I have spoken thus lightly, yet deep is the
   feeling that prompts me,
Surely you cannot refuse what I ask in the name of
   our friendship!'
Then made answer John Alden: 'The name of
   friendship is sacred;
What you demand in that name, I have not the power
   to deny you!'
So the strong will prevailed, subduing and moulding
   the gentler,
Friendship prevailed over love, and Alden went on his
   errand.

*From* THE COURTSHIP OF MILES STANDISH

### III.
### The Lover's Errand

So the strong will prevailed, and Alden went on his
errand.
Out of the street of the village, and into the paths of
the forest,
Into the tranquil woods, where bluebirds and robins
were building
Towns in the populous trees, with hanging gardens of
verdure,
Peaceful, aerial cities of joy and affection and freedom.
All around him was calm, but within him commotion
and conflict,
Love contending with friendship, and self with each
generous impulse.
To and fro in his breast his thoughts were heaving
and dashing,
As in a foundering ship, with every roll of the vessel,
Washes the bitter sea, the merciless surge of the ocean!
'Must I relinquish it all,' he cried with a wild
lamentation, –
'Must I relinquish it all, the joy, the hope, the illusion?
Was it for this I have loved, and waited, and
worshipped in silence?
Was it for this I have followed the flying feet and the
shadow

Over the wintry sea, to the desolate shores of New
  England?
Truly the heart is deceitful, and out of its depths of
  corruption
Rise, like an exhalation, the misty phantoms of
  passion;
Angels of light they seem, but are only delusions of
  Satan.
All is clear to me now; I feel it, I see it distinctly!
This is the hand of the Lord; it is laid upon me in
  anger,
For I have followed too much the heart's desires and
  devices,
Worshipping Astaroth blindly, and impious idols of Baal.
This is the cross I must bear; the sin and the swift
  retribution.'

So through the Plymouth woods John Alden went
  on his errand;
Crossing the brook at the ford, where it brawled over
  pebble and shallow,
Gathering still, as he went, the May-flowers blooming
  around him,
Fragrant, filling the air with a strange and wonderful
  sweetness,
Children lost in the woods, and covered with leaves in
  their slumber.
'Puritan flowers,' he said, 'and the type of Puritan
  maidens,

Modest and simple and sweet, the very type of Priscilla!
So I will take them to her; to Priscilla the May-flower
   of Plymouth,
Modest and simple and sweet, as a parting gift will I
   take them;
Breathing their silent farewells, as they fade and wither
   and perish,
Soon to be thrown away as is the heart of the giver.'
So through the Plymouth woods John Alden went on
   his errand;
Came to open space, and saw the disc of the ocean,
Sailless, sombre and cold with the comfortless breath
   of the east-wind;
Saw the new-built house, and the people at work in
   the meadow;
Heard, as he drew near the door, the musical voice of
   Priscilla
Singing the hundredth Psalm, the grand old Puritan
   anthem,
Music that Luther sang to the sacred words of the
   Psalmist,
Full of the breath of the Lord, consoling and
   comforting many.
Then, as he opened the door, he beheld the form of
   the maiden
Seated beside her wheel, and the carded wool like a
   snowdrift
Piled at her knee, her white hands feeding the
   ravenous spindle,

While with her foot on the treadle she guided the
wheel in its motion.
Open wide on her lap lay the well-worn psalm-book of
Ainsworth,
Printed in Amsterdam, the words and the music
together,
Rough-hewn, angular notes, like stones in the wall of a
churchyard,
Darkened and overhung by the running vine of the
verses.
Such was the book from whose pages she sang the old
Puritan anthem,
She, the Puritan girl, in the solitude of the forest,
Making the humble house and the modest apparel of
homespun
Beautiful with her beauty, and rich with the wealth of
her being!
Over him rushed, like a wind that is keen and cold
and relentless,
Thoughts of what might have been, and the weight
and woe of his errand;
All the dreams that had faded, and all the hopes that
had vanished,
All his life henceforth a dreary and tenantless
mansion,
Haunted by vain regrets, and pallid, sorrowful faces.
Still he said to himself, and almost fiercely he said it,
'Let not him that putteth his hand to the plough look
backwards;

Though the ploughshare cut through the flowers of life
 to its fountains,
Though it pass o'er the graves of the dead and the
 hearths of the living,
It is the will of the Lord; and his mercy endureth for
 ever!'

So he entered the house: and the hum of the wheel
 and the singing
Suddenly ceased; for Priscilla, aroused by his step on
 the threshold,
Rose as he entered, and gave him her hand, in signal
 of welcome,
Saying, 'I knew it was you when I heard your step in
 the passage;
For I was thinking of you, as I sat there singing and
 spinning.'
Awkward and dumb with delight, that a thought of
 him had been mingled
Thus in the sacred psalm, that came from the heart of
 the maiden,
Silent before her he stood, and gave her the flowers
 for an answer,
Finding no words for his thought. He remembered
 that day in the winter,
After the first great snow, when he broke a path from
 the village,
Reeling and plunging along through the drifts that
 encumbered the doorway,

Stamping the snow from his feet as he entered the
    house, and Priscilla
Laughed at his snowy locks, and gave him a seat by
    the fireside,
Grateful and pleased to know he had thought of her
    in the snowstorm.
Had he but spoken then! perhaps not in vain had he
    spoken;
Now it was all too late; the golden moment had
    vanished!
So he stood there abashed, and gave her the flowers
    for an answer.

Then they sat down and talked of the birds and the
    beautiful Spring-time,
Talked of their friends at home, and the May Flower
    that sailed on the morrow.
'I have been thinking all day,' said gently the Puritan
    maiden,
'Dreaming all night, and thinking all day, of the
    hedgerows of England, –
They are in blossom now, and the country is all like a
    garden;
Thinking of lanes and fields, and the song of the lark
    and the linnet,
Seeing the village street, and familiar faces of neighbours
Going about as of old, and stopping to gossip together,
And, at the end of the street, the village church, with
    the ivy

Climbing the old gray tower, and the quiet graves in
the churchyard.
Kind are the people I live with, and dear to me my
religion;
Still my heart is so sad, that I wish myself back in Old
England.
You will say it is wrong, but I cannot help it: I almost
Wish myself back in Old England, I feel so lonely and
wretched.'

Thereupon answered the youth: 'Indeed I do not
condemn you;
Stouter hearts than a woman's have quailed in this
terrible winter.
Yours is tender and trusting, and needs a stronger to
lean on;
So I have come to you now, with an offer and proffer
of marriage
Made by a good man and true, Miles Standish the
Captain of Plymouth!'

Thus he delivered his message, the dexterous writer
of letters, –
Did not embellish the theme, nor array it in beautiful
phrases,
But came straight to the point, and blurted it out like
a schoolboy;
Even the Captain himself could hardly have said it
more bluntly.

Mute with amazement and sorrow, Priscilla the Puritan
   maiden
Looked into Alden's face, her eyes dilated with wonder,
Feeling his words like a blow, that stunned her and
   rendered her speechless;
Till at length she exclaimed, interrupting the ominous
   silence:
'If the great Captain of Plymouth is so very eager to
   wed me,
Why does he not come himself, and take the trouble
   to woo me?
If I am not worth the wooing, I surely am not worth
   the winning!'
Then John Alden began explaining and smoothing the
   matter,
Making it worse as he went, by saying the Captain
   was busy, –
Had no time for such things; – such things! the words
   grating harshly
Fell on the ear of Priscilla; and swift as a flash she
   made answer:
'Has no time for such things, as you call it, before he
   is married,
Would he be likely to find it, or make it after the
   wedding?
That is the way with you men; you don't understand
   us, you cannot.
When you have made up your minds, after thinking of
   this one and that one,

Choosing, selecting, rejecting, comparing one with
    another,
Then you make known your desire, with abrupt and
    sudden avowal,
And are offended and hurt, and indignant perhaps,
    that a woman
Does not respond at once to a love that she never
    suspected,
Does not attain at a bound the height to which you
    have been climbing.
This is not right nor just: for surely a woman's affection
Is not a thing to be asked for, and had for only the
    asking.
When one is truly in love, one not only says it, but
    shows it.
Had he but waited awhile, had he only showed that
    he loved me,
Even this Captain of yours – who knows? – at last
    might have won me,
Old and rough as he is; but now it never can happen.'

Still John Alden went on, unheeding the words of
    Priscilla,
Urging the suit of his friend, explaining, persuading,
    expanding;
Spoke of his courage and skill, and of all his battles in
    Flanders,
How with the people of God he had chosen to suffer
    affliction,

How, in return for his zeal, they had made him
    Captain of Plymouth;
He was a gentleman born, could trace his pedigree
    plainly
Back to Hugh Standish of Duxbury Hall, in
    Lancashire, England,
Who was the son of Ralph, and the grandson of
    Thurston de Standish:
Heir unto vast estates, of which he was basely
    defrauded,
Still bore the family arms, and had for his crest a cock
    argent
Combed and wattled gules, and all the rest of the blazon.
He was a man of honour, of noble and generous
    nature;
Though he was rough, he was kindly; she knew how
    during the winter
He had attended the sick, with a hand as gentle as
    woman's;
Somewhat hasty and hot, he could not deny it, and
    headstrong,
Stern as a soldier might be, but hearty, and placable
    always,
Not to be laughed at and scorned, because he was
    little of stature;
For he was great of heart, magnanimous, courtly,
    courageous;
Any woman in Plymouth, nay, any woman in
    England,

Might be happy and proud to be called the wife of
  Miles Standish!

  But as he warmed and glowed, in his simple and
    eloquent language,
Quite forgetful of self, and full of the praise of his
  rival,
Archly the maiden smiled, and, with eyes overrunning
  with laughter,
Said, in a tremulous voice, 'Why don't you speak for
  yourself, John?'

# BECALMED

Becalmed upon the sea of Thought,
Still unattained the land is sought,
My mind, with loosely-hanging sails,
Lies waiting the auspicious gales.

On either side, behind, before,
The ocean stretches like a floor, –
A level floor of amethyst,
Crowned by a golden dome of mist.

Blow, breath of inspiration, blow!
Shake and uplift this golden glow!
And fill the canvas of the mind
With wafts of thy celestial wind.

Blow, breath of song! until I feel
The straining sail, the lifting keel,
The life of the awakening sea,
Its motion and its mystery!

# CHIMES

Sweet chimes! that in the loneliness of night
   Salute the passing hour, and in the dark
   And silent chambers of the household mark
   The movements of the myriad orbs of light!
Through my closed eyelids, by the inner sight,
   I see the constellations in the arc
   Of their great circles moving on, and hark!
   I almost hear them singing in their flight.
Better than sleep it is to lie awake
   O'er-canopied by the vast starry dome
   Of the immeasurable sky; to feel
The slumbering world sink under us, and make
   Hardly an eddy, – a mere rush of foam
   On the great sea beneath a sinking keel.

## FOUR BY THE CLOCK

Four by the clock! and yet not day;
But the great world rolls and wheels away,
With its cities on land, and its ships at sea,
Into the dawn that is to be!

Only the lamp in the anchored bark
Sends its glimmer across the dark,
And the heavy breathing of the sea
Is the only sound that comes to me.

# VOX POPULI

When Mazárvan the magician
  Journeyed westward through Cathay,
Nothing heard he but the praises
  Of Badoura on his way.

But the lessening rumour ended
  When he came to Khaledan,
There the folk were talking only
  Of Prince Camaralzaman.

So it happens with the poets:
  Every province hath its own;
Camaralzaman is famous
  Where Badoura is unknown.

# THE HAUNTED CHAMBER

Each heart has its haunted chamber,
  Where the silent moonlight falls!
On the floor are mysterious footsteps,
  There are whispers along the walls!

And mine at times is haunted
  By phantoms of the Past,
As motionless as shadows
  By the silent moonlight cast.

A form sits by the window,
  That is not seen by day,
For as soon as the dawn approaches
  It vanishes away.

It sits there in the moonlight,
  Itself as pale and still,
And points with its airy finger
  Across the window-sill.

Without, before the window,
  There stands a gloomy pine,
Whose boughs wave upward and downward
  As wave these thoughts of mine.

And underneath its branches
  Is the grave of a little child,
Who died upon life's threshold,
  And never wept nor smiled.

What are ye, O pallid phantoms!
  That haunt my troubled brain?
That vanish when day approaches,
  And at night return again?

What are ye, O pallid phantoms!
  But the statues without breath,
That stand on the bridge overarching
  The silent river of death?

# ON TRANSLATING THE DIVINA COMMEDIA

## First Sonnet

Oft have I seen at some cathedral door
   A labourer, pausing in the dust and heat,
   Lay down his burden, and with reverent feet
   Enter, and cross himself, and on the floor
Kneel to repeat his paternoster o'er:
   Far off the noises of the world retreat;
   The loud vociferations of the street
   Become an undistinguishable roar.
So, as I enter here from day to day,
   And leave my burden at this minster-gate,
   Kneeling in prayer, and not ashamed to pray,
The tumult of the time disconsolate
   To inarticulate murmurs dies away,
While the eternal ages watch and wait.

## Second Sonnet

How strange the sculptures that adorn these towers;
    This crowd of statues, in whose folded sleeves
    Birds build their nests; while canopied with leaves
    Parvis and portal bloom like trellised bowers,
And the vast minster seems a cross of flowers!
    But fiends and dragons on the gargoyled eaves
    Watch the dead Christ between the living thieves,
    And, underneath, the traitor Judas lowers!
Ah! from what agonies of heart and brain
    What exultations trampling on despair,
    What tenderness, what tears, what hate of wrong,
What passionate outcry of a soul in pain,
    Uprose this poem of the earth and air,
    This mediæval miracle of song!

## Third Sonnet

I enter, and I see thee in the gloom
   Of the long aisles, O poet saturnine!
   And strive to make my steps keep pace with thine.
   The air is filled with some unknown perfume;
The congregation of the dead make room
   For thee to pass; the votive tapers shine;
   Like rooks that haunt Ravenna's groves of pine
   The hovering echoes fly from tomb to tomb.
From the confessionals I hear arise
   Rehearsals of forgotten tragedies
   And lamentations from the crypts below;
And then a voice celestial that begins
   With the pathetic words, 'Although your sins
   As scarlet be,' and ends with 'as the snow.'

## Fourth Sonnet

With snow-white veil and garments as of flame,
　　She stands before thee, who so long ago
　　Filled thy young heart with passion and the woe
　　From which thy song and all its splendours came;
And while with stern rebuke she speaks thy name,
　　The ice about thy heart melts as the snow
　　On mountain heights, and in swift overflow
　　Comes gushing from thy lips in sobs of shame.
Thou makest full confession; and a gleam,
　　As of the dawn on some dark forest cast,
　　Seems on thy lifted forehead to increase;
Lethe and Eunoe – the remembered dream
　　And the forgotten sorrow – bring at last
　　That perfect pardon which is perfect peace.

## Fifth Sonnet

I lift mine eyes, and all the windows blaze
　　With forms of Saints and holy men who died,
　　Here martyred and hereafter glorified;
　　And the great Rose upon its leaves displays
Christ's Triumph, and the angelic roundelays,
　　With splendour upon splendour multiplied;
　　And Beatrice again at Dante's side
　　No more rebukes, but smiles her words of praise.
And then the organ sounds, and unseen choirs
　　Sing the old Latin hymns of peace and love
　　And benedictions of the Holy Ghost;
And the melodious bells among the spires
　　O'er all the house-tops and through heaven above
　　Proclaim the elevation of the Host!

## Sixth Sonnet

O star of morning and of liberty!
  O bringer of the light, whose splendour shines
  Above the darkness of the Apennines,
  Forerunner of the day that is to be!
The voices of the city and the sea,
  The voices of the mountains and the pines,
  Repeat thy song, till the familiar lines
  Are footpaths for the thought of Italy!
Thy fame is blown abroad from all the heights,
  Through all the nations, and a sound is heard,
  As of a mighty wind, and men devout,
Strangers of Rome, and the new proselytes,
  In their own language hear thy wondrous word,
  And many are amazed and many doubt.

# PALINGENESIS

I lay upon the headland-height, and listened
To the incessant sobbing of the sea
  In caverns under me,
And watched the waves, that tossed and fled and glistened
Until the rolling meadows of amethyst
  Melted away in mist.

Then suddenly, as one from sleep, I started;
For round about me all the sunny capes
  Seemed peopled with the shapes
Of those whom I had known in days departed,
Apparelled in the loveliness which gleams
  On faces seen in dreams.

A moment only, and the light and glory
Faded away, and the disconsolate shore
  Stood lonely as before;
And the wild-roses of the promontory
Around me shuddered in the wind, and shed
  Their petals of pale red.

There was an old belief that in the embers
Of all things their primordial form exists,
  And cunning alchemists
Could re-create the rose with all its members
From its own ashes, but without the bloom,
  Without the lost perfume.

Ah me! What wonder-working, occult science
Can from the ashes in our hearts once more
    The rose of youth restore?
What craft of alchemy can bid defiance
To time and change, and for a single hour
    Renew this phantom-flower?

'Oh, give me back,' I cried, 'the vanished splendours,
The breath of morn, and the exultant strife,
    When the swift stream of life
Bounds o'er its rocky channel, and surrenders
The pond, with all its lilies, for the leap
    Into the unknown deep!'

And the sea answered, with a lamentation,
Like some old prophet wailing, and it said,
    'Alas! thy youth is dead!
It breathes no more, its heart has no pulsation;
In the dark places with the dead of old
    It lies for ever cold!'

Then said I, 'From its consecrated cerements
I will not drag this sacred dust again,
    Only to give me pain;
But, still remembering all the lost endearments,
Go on my way, like one who looks before,
    And turns to weep no more.'

Into what land of harvests, what plantations
Bright with autumnal foliage and the glow
    Of sunsets burning low;
Beneath what midnight skies, whose constellations
Light up the spacious avenues between
    This world and the unseen!

Amid what friendly greetings and caresses,
What households, though not alien, yet not mine,
    What bowers of rest divine;
To what temptations in lone wildernesses,
What famine of the heart, what pain and loss,
    The bearing of what cross!

I do not know; nor will I vainly question
Those pages of the mystic book which hold
    The story still untold,
But without rash conjecture or suggestion
Turn its last leaves in reverence and good heed,
    Until 'The End' I read.

# IN THE CHURCHYARD AT CAMBRIDGE

In the village churchyard she lies,
Dust is in her beautiful eyes,
   No more she breathes, nor feels, nor stirs;
At her feet and at her head
Lies a slave to attend the dead,
   But their dust is white as hers.

Was she a lady of high degree,
So much in love with the vanity
   And foolish pomp of this world of ours?
Or was it Christian charity,
And lowliness and humility,
   The richest and rarest of all dowers?

Who shall tell us? No one speaks;
No colour shoots into those cheeks,
   Either of anger or of pride,
At the rude question we have asked;
Nor will the mystery be unmasked
   By those who are sleeping at her side.

Hereafter? – And do you think to look
On the terrible pages of that Book
   To find her failings, faults, and errors?
Ah, you will then have other cares,
In your own shortcomings and despairs,
   In your own secret sins and terrors!

# THE CROSS OF SNOW

In the long, sleepless watches of the night,
    A gentle face – the face of one long dead –
    Looks at me from the wall, where round its head
    The night-lamp casts a halo of pale light.
Here in this room she died; and soul more white
    Never through martyrdom of fire was led
    To its repose: nor can in books be read
    The legend of a life more benedight.
There is a mountain in the distant West
    That, sun-defying, in its deep ravines
    Displays a cross of snow upon its side.
Such is the cross I wear upon my breast
    These eighteen years, through all the changing scenes
    And seasons, changeless since the day she died.

# MY LOST YOUTH

Often I think of the beautiful town
    That is seated by the sea;
Often in thought go up and down
The pleasant streets of that dear old town.
    And my youth comes back to me,
        And a verse of a Lapland song
        Is haunting my memory still:
    'A boy's will is the wind's will,
And the thoughts of youth are long, long thoughts.'

I can see the shadowy lines of its trees,
    And catch, in sudden gleams,
The sheen of the far-surrounding seas,
And islands that were the Hesperides
    Of all my boyish dreams.
        And the burden of that old song,
        It murmurs and whispers still:
    'A boy's will is the wind's will,
And the thoughts of youth are long, long thoughts.'

I remember the black wharves and the slips,
    And the sea-tides tossing free;
And Spanish sailors with bearded lips,
And the beauty and mystery of the ships,
    And the magic of the sea.
        And the voice of that wayward song,
            Is singing and saying still:
        'A boy's will is the wind's will,
And the thoughts of youth are long, long thoughts.'

I remember the bulwarks by the shore,
    And the fort upon the hill;
The sunrise gun, with its hollow roar,
The drum-beat repeated o'er and o'er,
    And the bugle wild and shrill.
        And the music of that old song
            Throbs in my memory still:
        'A boy's will is the wind's will,
And the thoughts of youth are long, long thoughts.'

I remember the sea-fight far away,
    How it thundered o'er the tide!
And the dead captains, as they lay
In their graves, o'erlooking the tranquil bay,
    Where they in battle died.
        And the sound of that mournful song
            Goes through me with a thrill:
        'A boy's will is the wind's will,
And the thoughts of youth are long, long thoughts.'

I can see the breezy dome of groves,
   The shadows of Deering's Woods;
And the friendships old and the early loves
Come back with a Sabbath sound, as of doves
   In quiet neighbourhoods.
      And the verse of that sweet old song,
         It flutters and murmurs still:
      'A boy's will is the wind's will,
And the thoughts of youth are long, long thoughts.'


I remember the gleams and glooms that dart
   Across the schoolboy's brain;
The song and the silence in the heart,
That in part are prophecies, and in part
   Are longings wild and vain.
      And the voice of that fitful song
         Sings on, and is never still:
      'A boy's will is the wind's will,
And the thoughts of youth are long, long thoughts.'


There are things of which I may not speak;
   There are dreams that cannot die;
There are thoughts that make the strong heart weak,
And bring a pallor into the cheek,
   And a mist before the eye.
      And the words to that fatal song
         Come over me like a chill:
      'A boy's will is the wind's will,
And the thoughts of youth are long, long thoughts.'

Strange to me now are the forms I meet
    When I visit the dear old town;
But the native air is pure and sweet,
And the trees that o'ershadow each well-known street,
    As they balance up and down,
        Are singing the beautiful song,
        Are sighing and whispering still:
    'A boy's will is the wind's will,
And the thoughts of youth are long, long thoughts.'


And Deering's Woods are fresh and fair,
    And with joy that is almost pain
My heart goes back to wander there,
And among the dreams of the days that were,
    I find my lost youth again.
        And the strange and beautiful song,
        The groves are repeating it still:
    'A boy's will is the wind's will,
And the thoughts of youth are long, long thoughts.'

## SOMETHING LEFT UNDONE

Labour with what zeal we will,
  Something still remains undone,
Something uncompleted still
  Waits the rising of the sun.

By the bedside, on the stair,
  At the threshold, near the gates,
With its menace or its prayer,
  Like a mendicant it waits;

Waits, and will not go away;
  Waits, and will not be gainsaid;
By the cares of yesterday
  Each to-day is heavier made;

Till at length the burden seems
  Greater than our strength can bear,
Heavy as the weight of dreams,
  Pressing on us everywhere.

And we stand from day to day,
  Like the dwarfs of times gone by,
Who, as Northern legends say,
  On their shoulders held the sky.

## LOSS AND GAIN

When I compare
What I have lost with what I have gained,
What I have missed with what attained,
  Little room do I find for pride.

I am aware
How many days have been idly spent;
How like an arrow the good intent
  Has fallen short or been turned aside.

But who shall dare
To measure loss and gain in this wise?
Defeat may be victory in disguise;
  The lowest ebb is the turn of the tide.

# MEMORIES

Oft I remember those whom I have known
   In other days, to whom my heart was led
   As by a magnet, and who are not dead,
   But absent, and their memories overgrown
With other thoughts and troubles of my own,
   As graves with grasses are, and at their head
   The stone with moss and lichens so o'erspread,
   Nothing is legible but the name alone.
And is it so with them? After long years,
   Do they remember me in the same way,
   And is the memory pleasant as to me?
I fear to ask; yet wherefore are my fears?
   Pleasures, like flowers, may wither and decay,
   And yet the root perennial may be.

## MY BOOKS

Sadly as some old mediaeval knight
   Gazed at the arms he could no longer wield,
   The sword two-handed and the shining shield
   Suspended in the hall, and full in sight,
While secret longings for the lost delight
   Of tourney or adventure in the field
   Came over him, and tears but half concealed
   Trembled and fell upon his beard of white,
So I behold these books upon their shelf,
   My ornaments and arms of other days;
   Not wholly useless, though no longer used,
For they remind me of my other self,
   Younger and stronger, and the pleasant ways
   In which I walked, now clouded and confused.

# DEDICATION

## To G. W. G.

With favouring winds, o'er sunlit seas,
We sailed for the Hesperides,
The land where golden apples grow;
But that, ah! that was long ago.

How far, since then, the ocean streams
Have swept us from that land of dreams,
That land of fiction and of truth,
The lost Atlantis of our youth!

Whither, ah, whither? Are not these
The tempest-haunted Hebrides,
Where sea-gulls scream, and breakers roar
And wreck and seaweed line the shore?

Ultima Thule! Utmost Isle!
Here in thy harbours for a while
We lower our sails; a while we rest
From the unending, endless quest.